✫ ✫ ✫

Today

I Am

a Boy

✫ ✫ ✫

DAVID HAYS

Jenoa — What? You did this on time? Do it again in 55 years —

✫ ✫ ✫

SIMON & SCHUSTER

NEW YORK LONDON TORONTO SYDNEY SINGAPORE

David May 2001

SIMON & SCHUSTER
Rockefeller Center
1230 Avenue of the Americas
New York, NY 10020

Simon & Schuster and colophon are registered trademarks
of Simon & Schuster, Inc.

Book design by Ellen R. Sasahara

Manufactured in the United States of America

1   3   5   7   9   10   8   6   4   2

Library of Congress Cataloging-in-Publication Data
Hays, David.
Today I am a boy / David Hays
p.   cm.
1. Hays, David—Religion. 2. Jews—Connecticut—
Chester (Town)—Biography. 3. Bar mitzvah. I. Title.
F105.J5 H394 2000
296'.092—dc21
[B]   00-033905
ISBN 0-7432-0126-4

Acknowledgments

✳   ✳   ✳

With gratitude to Leonora, Julia and Jack, Dan and
Wendy, to Jesse and Jordan and you too, Jed, to Stephan
and to Laine Dyer and Doug May, Edith Exton, Linda
Meyer, Starr Sayres, Gene and Joyce Lasko, David
and Marion Bicks, Hal and Liz Lorin, Lou Connick,
Elaine Coleman, Eileen Dulin, Peter Walker,
Debbie Trautmann, JoAnn Price, Cory Weiss,
Ivan and Joyce Schmidt and Michael Posnick.

And to Bella Linden, Robert Gottlieb, Martha Kaplan,
Andrew Jakabovics, Gypsy da Silva, Jane Rosenman and
David Rosenthal, and Robert Rubin.

And to my new angels, Patricia Zipprodt,
Peter Feller and Betty Cage.

For Rabbi Doug

And to Lary Bloom, Joanne Greenberg,
and the Hormone Hurricanes

Contents

*   *   *

✵ ✵ ✵

TODAY
I AM
A BOY

✵ ✵ ✵

Chapter 1

✻ ✻ ✻

THE LUNCH BOX

A NY SMALL TOWN should have its Lunch Box, appropriate and inevitable. Ours opens between five and five-thirty in the morning and closes sometime after lunch. I walk to it early each day, and in winter's darkness I see ahead its warm light cast onto the street, turning exhaust from the idling pickups into amber steam that veils the golden retrievers and black Labs patiently waiting in the truck beds. Any such place must be a bit too small, have no waitress (you go to the counter), and preferably have no booths, because privacy spoils the mood. The opinions of the proprietress are unclouded. She knows about most of our affairs, and she cares about us. In my town this is the official Democratic Headquarters, but that discourages no Republican from hanging out here. A red-white-and-blue ribbon hangs in the window a few days before an election. The bulletin board is useful, displaying local services and events, and over it is a computer strip that says "Remember, you heard it first at the Lunch Box." The National Theatre of the Deaf makes its home in this town, and a

thoughtful patron has written "saw" under "heard." Sports and local matters are the topics called out between the tables in the early
morning. National concerns don't air before nine, but lively inter-
table action has tapered off long before, soon after seven. There are
distinct waves of patrons: my crowd—five-thirty to six-thirty—is
blue-collars, retirees who enjoy routine, and a man we might call
"challenged" who arrives every morning at exactly six-eleven and
reads the sports with the paper only an inch from his nose. His
knowledge of the schedules and statistics is encyclopedic and
loudly stated. In this early crowd we have coffee-for-the-car Hartford commuters and one artist who drops in for his paper and
doesn't take coffee. This is his morning walk. His dog, a border col-
lie, waits outside. In small towns we know people from a distance
by what they are driving or what they are walking. A corner table
by the window was always occupied by the town patriarch, and for
weeks after his death no one sat there. A monument to him was set
out on the table: the opener for his favorite beer, an empty bottle of
his bourbon, a basket containing a melon and some of those marvelous zucchinis and a ripe tomato to remind us of his garden's
bounty, which he shared with all of us. An artfully draped Italian
flag and a racing form completed the still life.

The newspapers arrive about six-fifteen—later on Thursdays,
which is unexplained—and when they do, many in the early crowd
read one and return it to the rack. Not much happens between
nine and noon except quick late breakfasts or coffee breaks, and
perhaps our dentist drops in, borrowing a paper and slowly sip-
ping coffee between appointments. The lunchers are workmen,
who take out meatball grinders, and some white-collar patrons
who have informal business lunches that tend toward the maca-
roni and cheese. When Charlene decides to thaw out a few stuffed

peppers, anyone in town might tell me that good news the day before. At lunch you can be left alone or sighted through the big windows and pinned flat like an insect and annoyed with someone else's problem, or worse, your own. You meet tradesmen and make appointments for work to be done, ranging from a new roof to computer counseling. I can leave a message with Charlene, or Darlene, second-in-command, or whoever told me about the stuffed peppers, for the dentist or anyone else to phone me when they come in. You don't really meet people at the Lunch Box, you run into them.

Perhaps it's because of the Lunch Box, the delivery room of journeys, where each day is born, that I'm sitting in a tiny classroom with eight twelve-year-olds, learning Hebrew.

I ran into our rabbi, young Doug Sagal, at the Lunch Box on an April morning in 1996 and told him that I was thinking more and more about studying to be a bar mitzvah. I can turn my mind to it because some of my duties at the theater have eased. "*Great!* Hebrew is an easy language," he says. "Just twenty-two letters. Lend me your pen." He draws a short straight line on the margin of the newspaper. "Say 'Ah.'" I say "Ah." "*Good!*" He draws two dots. "Say "'Eh.'" I say "Eh." "*Excellent!* David, there are five vowels, and you already know two of them! Let's start. Next Tuesday at ten?"

So we start. I can't remember exactly why I joined the small local congregation. When we lived in New York City I suggested that our son, Daniel, might go to Hebrew school, and my wife, Leonora, agreed. She investigated and reported that we'd have to join a temple and that ended the idea. There was too much going on, too little tradition in our upbringings to give a real sense of importance to this training. Daniel didn't complain, nor had I when I didn't go to Hebrew school. My brother, Richard, attended, and my theory is that he was such a scamp that my parents had no energy left for me. He was a lively boy; I remember my mother's distress when he was asked to leave Miss Chasen's piano classes. Richard doesn't remember much about his bar mitzvah. In that ferociously Reform "church" it may have been pale. He doesn't know how or why I evaded the training and ceremony. When I asked him recently, he paused and then said that he distinctly remembered a conversation in which Mom wondered whether I was Jewish.

How sexist our consideration now appears: what about our daughter? But bat or bas mitzvah, for girls, was relatively new, and unknown to us. The heart of our thinking may have been our theater work, which engulfed us and seemed to leave out nothing. It served as a Jewish community, Broadway, a hectic fascinating world veneered with Jewishness: peppered with Yiddish and with the testy shrugs and eye-rolling and sense of the frail mortality of the shows we brought to life and cared about. The small intense industry had the sense of a village craft, a sense of shtetl. When people with whom we shared our hearts, designers like Ray Sovey, Fred Voelpel and Patricia Zipprodt, were found out to be not Jewish, it was to our amazement and even to theirs. Indeed, when Toho wanted to originate an American musical in Tokyo, they chose what they believed to be Broadway's finest: Harold Rome, Joe Layton, Meyer Kupferman, Trudy Rittman and—I blush for the inclusion—myself. Only Patton Campbell, who designed the beautiful costumes, was, well, the name says it. So we called it a Japanese-Jewish musical.

. . .

Years went by. Why did we join a congregation here in Chester? Perhaps it was because the theater we had started had broken away from another Connecticut organization and moved here, and in this new community, in an area associated with the *Mayflower* (Essex, Old Lyme), I was surprised to find a lively Jewish world. In this new home, years away from New York, I may have wanted to renew a sense of that older family.

A young woman was rabbi at my new synagogue, and I liked her and enjoyed the services. This was my first real rabbi experience since I was eight, in 1938, witnessing my father's impatience with a rabbi's wife who was a frantic petitioner for her dull husband, helping him to keep his job. I don't count my wedding because that man talked forever and, as Leonora said, "I zeroed out." Now work took our rabbi's new husband from our small town to a big city abroad, and she went with him. Shortly after, I spoke at a graduation. A distinguished rabbi was to give the invocation, and as we waited to glide magnificently down the aisle, I told him of our search and said that our rabbi's replacement would probably be male. I said, "The thought of a man rabbi makes my flesh crawl." He threw his head back and laughed. "What's really so funny, David," he said, "is that you've just said a sentence that I'm sure has never been uttered in four thousand years."

So Doug came to us, not thirty years old, and the involvement of the congregants zoomed, and the number of families and singles zoomed, and the number of kids in Hebrew school zoomed plus one—me. "The Annex," where I'm to meet Doug, is rented for the Hebrew school. It's the upper floor of a three-shop minimall, where the main business is a dry cleaners owned by a delightful large family who came here from Sicily. They are Seventh Day Adventists and keep kosher, and they explain that to me. How appropriate this space is for me. I spent a year in graduate school at Yale, and four of us lived in an attic apartment above the Blue Jay Cleaners. The dry-cleaning aroma heralds a return to formal study. Our annex has a space as you enter that is big enough for seventy chairs. Offices and tiny classrooms converted from offices line up along the left side and fill the far end.

For my first lesson with Rabbi Doug I've already borrowed my grandson Jesse's beginning Hebrew workbook, and I know some letters. Jesse explained the instructions I have to follow. We noticed that his instructions are not exactly the same as mine. So what should I have expected? Any Jewish holiday, particularly Passover, is a long and usually pleasant argument. I wonder if *The Last Supper,* which was surely a Passover Seder, was full of spirited dispute about what could be cut from the long ceremony, when you drank the wine, what was the exact symbolism of the special foods, and when, please, can we start to eat? Who asked the four questions? Interesting questions, the four aspects of each of us. Alas, Leonardo's mural doesn't show children racing around the table. Brueghel should have painted it. On the subject, Leonora was told that she was named after the Beethoven heroine, but after a trip to Europe, her mother, Margaret, born in Hungary, told me how much she enjoyed the paintings "by Leonora da Vinci." When this loving woman died, her mantle of malapropisms fell on Leonora's shoulders.

Leonora is a woman of remarkable talents and a keen searching mind. Her specialty is compassion, not science. To illustrate this: she was deeply concerned for the astronauts, when they landed on the moon, that it should be a full moon. Her particular gifts are her artistry, for she was a fine, fine dancer, and her patience and loving support for family and people in general. That includes me, thrice blessed. Her malapropisms, or "Leonorisms," are not the result of foolishness, never that. Sometimes her mind goes faster than her mouth, sometimes her mouth goes faster than her mind. Her best sayings claim new linguistic territory, bringing forth phrases that enrich our language. "They moved to the country, but kept a pieta in town" is merely funny, but "It's still the women who take it on the brunt" blazes a new trail.

Finally, in Rabbi Doug's crowded office, I have my first Hebrew lesson, with coffee in Styrofoam. I'm learning from a man younger than my son, a man whose hobby is boxing. Your average boxing rabbi. We should have a rabbinical Olympics, maybe we'd be surprised; and I try to imagine the blow-by-blow commentary in the light-heavyweight division. "No hitting below the beard!" Doug's teaching is encouraging at every turn. This will be a no-lose situation. "*Yes!*" he says when I get the pronunciation almost right. "*Yes, Almost!*" when I get it wrong. Jesse's workbook is good, he explains, but maybe this one—take mine, he says—will be better for you. I am to study the first eight lessons. I leave elated.

Leonora says, "He's hooked, line and sinker!"

Chapter 2

✳   ✳   ✳

THE HIVES

I'VE ALREADY LEARNED that you can't mess around higgledy-piggledy with the great mysteries. I've not learned this in my studies with Doug but in the after-hours reading about my people that is taking more and more of my time. I read in a book about mysticism that one must not peek unprepared into the high chambers. One might fast for some days, then place one's head between one's knees and whisper into the ground many traditional songs and phrases. Even then, the story is told of four who entered the Orchard; one gazed and died, another was stricken . . . so beware. What I'm trying to do is to understand this mystery: why am I in this classroom? One answer is an event that took place almost two years before Rabbi Doug set my feet on the aleph-bet path.

When my mother died in 1992, my son, Dan, used his inheritance to buy an island named Whale Island off the eastern tip of Nova Scotia. It is rugged and beautiful, not overly expensive, because down there, at the south side of the ridge as the peninsula narrows, there might be only ten minutes of summer. The land thrills me, and the water is Bahama clear. The fogs dare me as I pilot our launch between rocks and steep-sided islands, threading along the coast to the small fishing town. We were building a small house for Dan, no more than a sturdy cabin, and he chose a magnificent but difficult site on a cliff six hundred winding and steep feet from the boat landing. It's the best place to see the dramatic weather patterns, which change swiftly as the fronts sweep in from the southwest. The mists are Japanese, and often we see only the tops of the short scrub spruce, pale sketches emerging from white rice paper.

Dan was at that time a wilderness guide, and he asked one of the other guides, an experienced carpenter I will call Charlie, to join us. Charlie would be paid for his work and be the steady hand through the four weeks of construction. Eager and less-skilled friends would join us for shorter periods.

Charlie was a not a total success. He worked hard, but spent hours sharpening fancy tools when the chain saw was our joinery standard. He wolfed down, alone, the treat foods we brought out to share, and when a young woman came out to help us, he wore a sweatshirt to dinner, which sounds mild, but he wore it with his legs thrust through the sleeves. Figure it out.

The real trouble was over the whale's teeth, and I was at some fault but not the villain. Two sperm whales, the larger one almost sixty feet long, had washed up on the island the year before and the flesh had rotted away. Actually the ice-caked corpses had drifted into the channel alongside the island, and the fishermen had pushed them onto our beach, not wanting the smell closer to their homes. They had taken the prized teeth, but one day Charlie was standing near the shore and looked down to see three six-inch teeth, the size you see etched to make scrimshaw. He brought them in to show us, and I whispered to him that I hoped he would give one to Dan.

The day Charlie was to leave us, I brought up the subject again, presenting the idea that it was Dan who had brought us out there and he would love such a prize, souvenir of Whale Island indeed. Charlie replied that he wanted to keep one and give one to his niece and one to his best friend. I said again that Dan had made this happen, didn't he think it an appropriate gesture to return just one of the three as a gift? Charlie said that, man, I was crowding him, he had to make his own decision. I said yes, though the teeth were actually Dan's property, found on his land. "Your decision," I said, "I'm suggesting strongly, but that's the end of it. And please don't draw Dan into this; it's our chat." In a few minutes I heard him call for Dan, and two minutes later Dan came to me as I was preparing the boat. "Dad, Charlie just said that he'd planned to give me a tooth but you crowded him so hard that now he won't." "What a lie," I said, and by the time Charlie was on board and ready to leave the harbor, I was steaming.

I had decided not to shave during our work time, and after four weeks I sported a white beard and looked about halfway between Michelangelo's *Moses* and Reuters' Yasir Arafat. I scrambled onto the boulder that served as our landing place and stretched a stern and trembling hand toward Charlie. One spectator mentioned later that I rose slightly from the rock. "I curse you!" I roared. "I curse you and your generations for this lie that you intended to come between a father and his son!" And so forth. It seemed effective. Charlie's knees shook, and he sat down hard in the boat. Daniel took him ashore, where he found that the off-road lights had been stolen from his truck, which he then backed into the dock, smashing its rear end. He drove down the road, swerving from side to side. The next morning I woke to a grand case of hives.

I have a photo of Dan and myself and Jesse, my daughter, Julia's, eldest, then six years old. It was taken by Jesse's father, Jack, on the day after the curse, cleanup day. We four had interrupted the cleaning, loading, and storing to celebrate my birthday. The photo was taken indoors so that you can see the candlelight—but it's not sharp, and you can't see the hives. What you see is Dan and me making wry faces to indicate that we understand the joke: the birthday cake is only a tiny cupcake, ha-ha. Jesse is carefully holding the cake, and his face is underlit by the single candle. He seems haloed, and he glows in the scene because he is not joking but is a respectful high priest of the awesome ceremony of birthday.

I presented this matter of the curse and the hives to Rabbi Doug at a chance meeting. I confessed that perhaps I hadn't been well enough prepared to deliver the curse. "Maybe I should have been a bar mitzvah," I said. Doug was noncommittal. Perhaps he wanted more time to think about it. The ramifications of a curse are not common in the town of Chester, Connecticut. But the idea of bar mitzvah, long dead in my mind, had been resurrected by the curse, had actually been mentioned out loud. There hung the glittering letters in the air between me and my rabbi, surrounded by an ornate gold frame. One can't reach out and stuff all that back in one's mouth.

I sent a note to Charlie telling him to feel free to drop me a postcard, anytime, describing how the curse was going, but I haven't heard from him. A year later he gave Dan one of the teeth.

Chapter 3

*　*　*

MY FIRST DAY AT SCHOOL

OUG GOES TO THE blackboard to show how Abraham
journeyed to the Holy Land. He draws a map of what is
basically today's Israel. It looks like New Jersey. He steps
back and looks at it. "It looks like New Jersey," he says.

Doug tells me that he believes. A rabbi certainly should. Why
does this make me pause to think? I know so many Jews who work
hard for Judaism in one way or another, who go to temple every
week, who know and enjoy the major prayers in Hebrew, and not
one truly believes in God. Is that what all of this is about for me,
questioning this, taking this journey at my age?

For me, conceiving of God has always been too hard, and perhaps I've made it hard because I seek for an image where one may
not be needed or possible. The painters I eagerly studied supply
images that become ingrained and hard to shake off. It is often expressed that God's image is the greatest barrier to Him. In Christianity, of course, there is a man-God to address. The concepts that

God is love, or all of nature, as expressed to me by friends with those beliefs, seem too simple to me: sensible, yet brush-offs. My uncertainty is common, and I'm not ashamed of it. But I do believe in angels, and they come from some source that is God. These angels are not to me the messengers who take on human form and change a tire when it's raining. That, as I read the airline magazines, is one common conception of heavenly helpers, and as meaningful to me as "Have a nice day." I have a friend who believes that any twenty-first-century person who believes in God just isn't paying attention. The same of course for our popular angels. "I go to the supermarket," he says, "a room so big it has its own weather. It's misty over here by produce but far across, above the pepperonis, it's clearing. There are perhaps twenty people—voting citizens!—in between. Fourteen of these believe in angels!!"

Recently, while sailing along the Maine coast, a fisherman in an outboard runabout materialized out of the thick fog and told us that we were about to hit mainland, pointed in the correct direction, and then vanished into the whiteness. An angel? I know people who believe that they merit God's minute attention, even when they're in yachts. No, this was a fisherman in an outboard runabout who didn't want to waste an hour of his time on crashed amateur sailors. If he were an angel I admire his props, well done and quickly assembled: a few days' stubble, a battered boat, an ancient outboard, dirty nets and buoys and lobster traps, a dangling half-smoked cigarette and a breath-stopping stink of lobster bait that preceded him out of the fog.

But I knew one angel. George Balanchine was an angel. I designed his sets and lighting for many years, and he was very much a man, a man who had weaknesses and did a number of ordinary things badly: his marriages were poorly managed, he cut off a finger with his lawn mower. He loved silly dirty jokes that we told backstage as we waited nervously with Ron Bates, our stage manager, for the curtain to go up on a new piece. But the work, the work, it flowed through him with a power that could not be explained by Darwin. It came through him as a force of music, compressed and refined to essences of movement, radiant with new vistas, illuminated, poured into our spirits. Now I learn in class that the Hebrew word *malach* means both "messenger" and "angel." That's what I mean. Suzanne Farrell was a kind of angel, Balanchine's angel, and above all of the great women he empowered, she was the seamless extension of his arm.

I don't pray to God for myself. I name friends who are sick. Whatever my current heavenly standing, I would be mortified to make requests, to insult Him or Her by asking for even more than has been given to me. I know I'm lucky. I know I don't endure the bitterness of those who see this glorious world but are barred from it by pain or poverty, or by the disappointment of what it offers and then snatches away. But I did pray once. My brother and I— was I six and he nine?—prayed for bulbs for our Lionel train switches. Standard gauge, the best of course, the old Blue Comet. We pulled down the shades; it must have been a winter afternoon because I remember the way the light burst into that west-facing attic room. Then in the dimmed playroom we lit a candle and prayed. I don't remember the words but I was terrified when Dad came home that night and brought the bulbs we needed. It required calming down over a few years before I even thought of the possibility that the topic had been mentioned at breakfast or later in the morning to Mom, who may have told Dad at their midday phone call. When at last I talked about it to Dad, he had no memory of that small part of one day, years behind him, and he only disappointed me by talking about his belief in "mental telepathy," as it was called then.

The incident didn't encourage me to pray for more toys or for any other thing I wanted. I was so overwhelmed by the power of prayer that I didn't dare use up whatever miraculous inventory, the other two wishes, that might have remained to me. Thinking back, I am impressed with my logic as a boy. Logic puts me off when supernatural powers are discussed; *if* they exist, I reason, our normal reasoning powers would by definition be worthless before them.

I get no enjoyment from the standard miracles such as walking on water, flaming bushes, etc. To put topsy-turvy the ordinary forces of gravity and such matters would be easy for the person who created gravity, if that's the drill. Showing a sleight-of-hand, manipulating those wonders, pales beside the wonders themselves.

These thoughts, some long forgotten, come back to me on a Sunday morning in early September, the first day of Hebrew school. I'm nervous, but Leonora speeds me off to school with, "Good luck. Just hang on, teeth and nail."

We are about sixty students, ranging in age from six to twelve, then the fifty-four-year jump to me. The chairs are full sized, so much for my worry of sitting on baby chairs with my knees up to my chin. We assemble and join hands and then sit, and each of us is given half a piece of paper inscribed with Hebrew letters in a decorated style that I cannot read until they are pronounced. We are told to close our eyes, and when we open them a small piece of candy, a Hershey's Kiss, is on the paper. "To show," says Rabbi Doug, "how sweet is the study of Torah." Sometimes, in jest, he pronounces it "Toirah," the Yiddish way. But the study can be hard, he points out.

The faculty, a dozen or so including apprentice teachers, give a brief improvised show that is funny enough, the musical chorus centered on the Hebrew word *moreh* or "teacher" (*morah* is the feminine form). Then we all stand and hold hands again and sing a song that every other kid seems to know.

Next, my class goes to our tiny classroom. One window, one eight-foot table, shelves, a bulletin board, paper things hung about—you know, you've been there. This room also has the school's supply closet, big enough so that a group of four students can shut themselves in it to prepare their half of a debate, meaning sounds of slaps and giggles. The closet also ensures that other teachers will come in and out during our class, squeezing by us to get to it. My pre–bar mitzvah/bas mitzvah group includes four boys and three girls. One boy is taller than me. All of the boys have bigger feet than mine, easily seen because they are usually arranged on the table, but who can tell actual size in these high sneakers, where the foot seems to vanish into a colorful garbage bag? Our teachers are Rabbi Doug and Debbie Trautmann, who is the daughter of a famous rabbi of the Reform movement, and she is younger than my daughter. Our work starts, clearly no holy quest but a gathering of lively conniving twelve-year-olds, eager to escape anything named "work," clearly to be full of release energy on our Wednesday afternoons and impatient to get on with the rest of the day on our Sunday mornings. They've been together for as many as six years. At first glance I'd have any of them for a child or grandchild.

I meet Aaron, Adam, Alex, Mark, Sara, Jami, and Rachel.

My appearance in class surprises them, but they are kind, and my presence doesn't seem to make them act any more or less attentive or rowdy. They don't show off to me. We read passages in English from a workbook designed to show us our responsibilities as

Jewish adults. We read Hebrew and play flash-card and other games. I'm slow, knowing neither the content nor the rules. But I'm too old to embarrass. Only my mother could do that, particularly in the supermarket when she was old and I took her there, where she would stand and eat from broken boxes of cookies ("They can't sell them anyway"). Once she *kvitched* so loudly because celery had gone up ten cents that a man walked over and gave this wealthy but shabbily dressed woman a dime, which she eagerly took. Maybe he was an angel.

Aaron is the tall boy, thin and quiet. He has an attractive and sweet shyness and doesn't horse around, as my generation used to say. He has huge spidery handwriting and weeks later, when I offer to show him how to do a blockier printing, he backs off quickly, and I feel insensitive and clumsy. There is a kindness in him, and I'm drawn to him. He remembers to pass me the snacks, because I don't grab at them the way the other kids do.

Adam is sturdy, blond, "cool"—and sexy, I learn, when the bar mitzvahs of this group begin in the spring. The girls, dressed up for the ceremony and the party afterward, tend to kick, pinch, and poke Adam as they squeeze past him in the aisle, heading (many times during the ceremony) for chatter in the ladies' room. Adam wears butch clothing and accessories such as a studded leather wrist band. I'm told that he's a talented musician, and I'm touched when I see that he's not ashamed, despite this tricky time in life, to publicly show affection to his mother, who is divorced. He can be sullen in class. Perhaps he's bored. Now his chair has fallen backward, and he's jammed under the bookshelf. His face is not visible, and he lost his balance because he was concentrating on pulling the collar of his leather jacket up over his face and then zipping it closed. His brush of yellow hair is visible where his neck should be.

Now that's gone too, because the collar of the jacket is snug up against the bottom of the shelf. If I could quickly cut out a face and put it on the shelf, it would seem correctly mounted on his neck. Whose face? Doug might be content with Attila the Hun, and we could reuse it for most of these kids. "America's Future Most Wanted," he calls them. He persists, asking Adam to read. Adam replies that it's dark and he can't see. Juvenile hilarity rocks the room.

Sara is tall for her age, attractive, loves bizarre fingernail painting, loves to talk, loves to bait the boys, and is starting to feel that power over them that girls can feel at that age. She has a passion for Rabbi Doug and takes outrageous liberties, such as lifting his *kippah* (yarmulke) to peer at his hairline. She can barely keep her hands off him and that boldness, though innocent, raises her position in the group. She's not shy with me and includes me in conversation.

I have a theory, which I later express to Doug, that these kids are growing so fast that each week they see more of the top of his head, which is why they keep track of his increasing forehead. Doug will buy any theory about his receding hair.

Alex is a boy I will never get to know. He is on a special soccer team and is often absent. He is quick and knows his lessons, and it isn't until later in the year that he will participate in the politically correct and required rebellion against our teachers. Doug accepts this as a part of the growth toward the ceremony. There is a theory, he tells me after class, that Adam and Eve were teenagers, and that their rebellion was mankind's first enactment of these perplexing years. Alex's bar mitzvah will be the first, in the spring.

Doug demonstrates the ram's horn, the shofar, that will be blown at the upcoming holidays to summon the penitents. This can be the horn of any kosher animal: sheep, goat, gazelle, or antelope, but not that of a cow or an ox because of the Golden Calf idolatry. That idolatry, however, didn't stop us from eating cattle. I remember buying a shofar to be used in a play, forty years ago, before Doug was born. Forty years is the time Moses spent in the desert. It goes by quickly. I understand that I haven't achieved as much.

On Sundays the whole school meets from nine-thirty to twelve-fifteen or so: seven classes, ages six through twelve. Debbie will be our teacher on Sundays. Doug will conduct our Wednesday afternoon sessions, from four to five-thirty. Wednesdays are for the two oldest classes, gearing up for graduation, which means the bar or bat mitzvah ceremonies.

On this first day of class we split up a cake that announces the start of the year's study. Then I learn that the real name of God is not mentioned. "The Lord" is one substitution. One of Doug's teachers wrote one half of the actual name on one side of the room and the rest of it on the other. In our translation of the Torah it is indicated as YHWH and pronounced, though rarely, "Yahweh," or "Yahveh," like an expiration of breath. Some people even fake "God" with "G__D," which seems a mild heresy to me. My mother, for example, wouldn't be fooled by forbidden words spelled out with dashes. Doug later shows me a note from one of his younger students. It says, "I don't believe in G__D."

We answer Doug's question about how we will feel after bar mitzvah and as we grow older. Overwhelmingly, the anticipated reward is *freedom*. No longer bossed around, no longer a second-rate citizen. Maybe our opinions will finally be respected by those adults who think they are so superior to us. But Jami points out that the teen years are the toughest, so don't be so sure that your status will be instantly upgraded. Adam says that he'll be able to come to synagogue when he wants to, not when he's told to. Sure, says Sara, if someone drives him. We end at noon, just as lively spirits become too much for the small classroom.

At my private session with Doug on the next Tuesday, he tells me that I should keep a good eye on these kids. They're going to change so much this year, and I'll be fascinated. I'm excited by this. I like them and I like our teachers.

When I told my friend Lary Bloom, who is a writer and editor, that I wanted to study Hebrew and be a bar mitzvah but I'd be damned if I'd sit in class with twelve-year-olds, he said, "Oh yes you will," sensing a story. Leonora added that she'd like to be a fly on the wallpaper. Now I understand that if this alone is what is in store, if nothing more will come from this enterprise than to sit with these kids, to learn again with young people, even if they are ahead of me and smarter to boot, why, that would be enough.

Chapter 4

* * *

MY MOTHER WAS NEVER WRONG

PERHAPS THERE IS a pilgrimage gene in our DNA. Perhaps when my mother died I longed for a special journey, a symbolic journey. Repentance? No reason for that, I was a good son, nor was there any specificity of sadness for the death of a ninety-four-year-old woman. But I may have had a strange guilt because I could no longer take care of her. Is that another irrational reason that has placed me in a small classroom with children of my grandson's generation? Am I rerunning a lap that I didn't complete more than a half-century ago, when I was twelve? Am I surging forward again in the race that my mother coached and cheered?

The starting pistol for my mother's own last lap was fired in a diner in Stamford, Connecticut. It was not the sound of a shot or a rumble on the kettle drums, but in my imagination it is that haunting sound in the distant forest or sky in *The Cherry Orchard,* the unexplained sound of a breaking string, mournfully dying away, and the land will be swept away and the people will be swept away, as was my mother with the loss of her house and her treasured sunsets. The path to my mother's death was the start of my own journey now, the generational relay race, the overlapping motion of people like myself who are orphaned late in their lives.

. . .

Mom doesn't like the small city of Stamford. "Humph, Stamford, what does it think it is?!" We are sitting in a booth with her brother Eddie, who is about seventy-eight. Mom is eighty-four. It's just before noon in this fancified place, neo–Castro Convertible, a grounded flight of fancy. Mom doesn't like it. Eddie does, this is his hangout. He is the particular friend of an elderly man with no teeth at all who mops and takes out the garbage. Eddie and he have a secret code. "Tom Sawyer," says Eddie when he leaves. "Tom Sawyer," says his friend indistinctly, and giggles. It's not hard to break the code. *Sayonara* means good-bye in Japanese. This is the peak of wit and social intercourse for Eddie, although sometimes he says "Tempus fidgets."

Eddie was an infantryman in the Second World War and fought well, I've been told. He then became a bureaucrat in the Veterans Administration and had responsibilities in Connecticut. He traveled back and forth across the state in various Buicks and lived in various YMCAs. Once, with a girlfriend, he bought a crumbling bed-and-breakfast and sped its failure. The girlfriend disappeared after she was not invited to a family wedding. "She just got fed up," my mother said. Then for two years, when he was about seventy-five, Eddie lived with Mom in her big house in Norwalk. He lived in a room and bath intended for a servant, off the kitchen. My mother hated his cans of carbonated soft drinks that polluted her refrigerator, but what was unbearable to her were Eddie's talcum-powder footprints that entered from his room, wandered the spotless kitchen linoleum and then exited. Eddie wasn't happy because he wanted a shower in his bathroom and Mom wouldn't rig one because she felt that the tub was quite enough. Eddie countered that sitting in hot water lowered his sperm count. Mom saw no merit in that argument for a seventy-five-year-old bachelor, and Eddie departed to revitalize his parts. Now he lives in a small apartment in Stamford near the elegant retirement home Mom has recently entered. The diner is in neutral territory, two blocks from each residence. Mom has called this meeting, Eddie doesn't yet know why, and I'm just the transportation. My brother, Richard, can't be here because he's in a hospital recovering from a heart bypass operation. He's being tended there by his wife, Sue.

We are seated in a booth. Mom's gnarled fingers are like talons, clenched on the table rim so tightly that she seems perched, and when she leans forward, with the intensity and mien of the witch in *Snow White,* she might have no lower body at all, but be a hawk or a condor clutching a limb. Yet Mom is beautiful, and she changes magically and flows with youth when she laughs. But, "Today's business is no laughing matter," she warned me on the way over.

Eddie sits back, waiting for the attack. He knows the signs. No intensity here: his face is like a tentative sketch, a lay-in of pink without the lines and highlights to snap it up, a Hallmark face, a background-crowd face. He also knows as I do that Mom is never wrong. I don't write that with my tongue in my cheek. I simply have no memory of Mom ever having to retreat from any of life's skirmishes. Aware of her gift, Mom was impatient with those who challenged her, and considered any defense a waste of her time. She was right, of course. Her technique aimed at the foolish questioner was what my brother and I called "Repetition in Crescendo." It worked simply. An example: for many years I heard her say, "If you're a Jew you give—*or else.*" Finally I asked, "Or else what, Mom?" "*OR ELSE!!*" Simple as that. Now Mom begins.

"Eddie, I just visited Ben Alk at Courtland Gardens. They do everything for him. You should move there."

"Why?"

"Because you're getting forgetful."

"So what?"

"You don't pay your rent."

"I pay my rent."

"No you don't—or you pay it twice."

"I don't remember that."

"That's exactly what I mean! You don't remember!"

"How do you know that?"

"I just know!"

"I'm happy where I am."

"But they're not happy with you!"

"Who told you that?"

"Your landlady—David, order fruit cup—is not happy."

"Who's complaining?"

"Your landlady."

"Who did she complain to?"

"To Sue, and Sue told Richard here. Richard, try the fruit cup."

"What did she complain about?"

"Eddie, your room is a mess."

"Did you ever see it?"

"I drove over one day with Richard or David, I don't remember which. Anyway, you weren't there. We didn't go in."

"I don't remember that."

"How could you? You weren't there. And that's exactly what I'm talking about! Look, Eddie, this isn't so terrible, you shouldn't be upset."

"I'm not upset."

"Well, you should be!"

"What's the complaint?"

"See! You don't remember."

"Oh, Sadie, there's nothing worth remembering anymore."

"That's ridiculous."

"I'm happy where I am."

"But they're not happy with you."

"Who said so?"

"Your landlady."

"Did she tell you?"

"No, she told Sue, and Sue told Richard. Richard, have the fruit cup."

"Mom, I've finished it."

"Why does my landlady tell other people and not me?"

"Because she knows she'll never get anywhere with you."

"So who did she complain to?"

"To Leonora, and Leonora told David here."

"How did she know Leonora's name?"

"Leonora has nothing to do with this. She told Sue."

"How did she get Sue's name?"

"She didn't call Sue. She called Richard."

"Why?"

"Because your apartment's a mess and she's worried about you."

"Why? I pay the rent."

"You paid it twice last month."

"I must have gotten a refund."

"You don't remember, do you? Eddie, Courtland Gardens is a good place. They have meals and there's a hospital nearby."

"But I like to eat out."

"You can't eat out three times a day."

"I don't eat three times a day."

"Yes you do."

"No, in the morning I just have juice and coffee."

"And lunch?"

"I don't eat lunch."

"You don't?"

"No, I just have juice and coffee."

"What about breakfast?"

"I don't eat breakfast."

"Look, Eddie, the time has come. You should go to Courtland Gardens."

"I saw it once. I thought it was expensive."

"You can afford it, can't you?"

"In a way I can and in a way I can't."

"You can't take it with you, Eddie."

"I have a bedroom and a living room where I have a chair."

"Well, you're impossible."

"Of course I am, but I'm happy where I am. You know, I fought through Germany all during the war. Nothing happened to me."

"I know."

"How did you know that?"

"You told me. Now you've got to think of moving. I'll call and see how much Courtland Gardens costs. You can have your meals there."

"But I like to eat out."

"Maybe we'll visit there."

"I saw it once but it was too expensive."

"What's too expensive?"

"I forget."

"See! You forget everything!"

"It's better not to remember, Sadie."

"Richard, did you eat your fruit cup?"

At about the arrival of the fruit cup I realized that this was to be no ordinary court-martial of a younger brother and that it would make my own brother laugh. I took notes. After I drove Mom home I went on to New Haven to visit him. He sat raised on the hospital bed, tethered and tubed and in obvious discomfort. "Where are your kids?" I asked, and Sue told me that Richard didn't want them to see him suffer. I said that when I have *my* bypass my kids damn well will see me suffer, and shoulder as much grief as I can off-load onto them, and this is what happened six years later, adding to their pleasure as loving family members and speeding my recovery. The hospital refused to let them watch or help at the operating table, but they were with me at every possible other time. My brother was depressed at having to undergo his surgery, but when it was my turn I was elated. If only this procedure, which would extend my life, had been invented in time for my father.

My brother and I are different people. Not such a simple statement, and I was sixty-five before a lifelong friend, older than both of us, pointed this out. I was confiding that we didn't always get along, and Al Alk, Ben's son, suggested that this hurt me because I assumed that my older hero-brother and I were the same, and that any dispute must be more than half my fault. "Stuff that; you were so very different as kids and you're different now," he said. Anyway, we can make each other laugh, and I did that for him in the hospital as I read my transcript of the Stamford Massacre.

There was more to it than that, I realized years later. The reason I call it the start of Mom's final journey, and therefore mine, was because she was reaching out to Eddie. Her house, her land, was gone, she was disconnected and going down, and she wanted company. She was groping to pull him along with her. He wouldn't be the best traveling companion for her, a man who said that it's better not to remember, a man who had a living room with a chair. When I put Eddie into a home two years later, her sense of solitary decline was eased, but by the time Eddie died, three years before Mom, she was looking beyond him and toward her own mother.

Chapter 5

* * *

MY FIRST FIELD TRIP

LEX'S NOTEBOOK IS neater than mine, but I marvel at the destructive zeal of the other kids, peeling the plastic lamination from the notebook covers. As with blue jeans, torn is "in," and "scribbled on" seems essential. I remember when Pocket Books were first published in this country during World War Two, when I was a teen. They had a cellophany coating on their covers that was easy to pick off, as engrossing an activity as peeling your sunburn or picking at those rubber circles on the backs of your Keds. If you were careful, that could last the whole summer.

When I was a kid the trick was to be outrageous when the teacher's back was turned, when he or she was writing on the blackboard. Notes or spitballs could be thrown, and one could leap up and make funny faces, but in silence. This took skill and nerve, a game of chicken that stopped on a dime when the teacher turned around to face the class, like the school-yard game Red Light. Today it's a different kind of nerve that's needed, because the peer points the kids earn are for being sassy or obstructive right in the teacher's face. It shocks me. "How the hell do you put up with that, Doug?" "Because, David, I will win in the end. I always do. They will respect the ceremony, they will be glad, they'll be grateful. Watch. Time and terror will do it."

I learn more about my classmates. Mark is alert and knowledgeable about his lessons and much else, with wild and forceful opinions about anything, particularly prejudice in any form, which he cannot bear to the point that he is madly prejudiced himself for the good cause. He feels at ease with me and is encouraging. He has trouble not talking in class, and with his longtime friend Sara creates the longest interruptions to classwork. He is handsome and bears an unsettling resemblance to my cardiologist, looking perhaps only a month younger.

Jami is attractive also, with olive skin and eyes that are dark brown, almost black. Something drives her deep into her shell, and when Doug or Debbie asks her to participate in any way, for example, to read a passage in Hebrew, they have to reel her to the surface. Sometimes she simply says "No," and it takes patience to change that, but it's worth it. She reads beautifully. She will comment at any time in class, and she can be funny. "Rabbi Doug, why are you obsessed with that prayer?" She knows her Hebrew well and is smart and alert behind her moods, and she has a special and keen ability to root out the meaning of a symbol or passage. When she suddenly looks straight at you, she has a stunning, snap-eyed personal force.

A big moment in any class is snacktime. On Wednesdays this happens toward the end of class, when we, mostly Doug, speak only Hebrew. We call it Hebrew *hoog*. The Rice Krispies stuck in marshmallow are Doug's favorite, a hard part of the afternoon for me. But the Pringles are great. Aaron brings the best snacks. "Yeah," smirks Adam, "he tells his mother that you require them, Rabbi." Today Doug tells one of his favorite stories, about the respected rabbi who disappeared for a day every year, just before the High Holy Days. One year he was followed and was seen, not ascending to the angels, but merely chopping wood for a poor old widow. Maybe he is flying higher than the angels, said the observers.

On Rosh Hashanah Eve, John DeNicola, our lay cantor, a young man who is a composer and who converted from Catholicism, sings beautifully. We also have fine singing from Harriet Fellows, our president, who took lessons when a girl because she wanted to be near the teacher's son, her heartthrob. Doug also sings well. Jews sing their Bible. I didn't even realize that. I believe that we are unique in this way of reciting the Bible. Then Doug gives a fine sermon about three processions that meet at a crossroad: that of the king, a bridal party, a funeral. Who gets right-of-way? This is the kind of question that can fill volumes of the Talmud. In one classic solution, the king uses his authority and gives the nod to the wedding. I tell Doug afterward that I would let the king do the nodding, but I would choose the corpse. It's the deceased's final curtain call and deserves our respect. I'm not a scholar, but I have Doug's respect in this, and I can dispute the point and join the questioning generations. Plenty of Jews have better credentials to argue this, but none has more right.

During the service, Doug talks of our diversity in this synagogue: rich and poor, straight and gay, Jew and gentile. He forgot black, and we have black members. We have many mixed marriages, and Lary Bloom jokes to me that we are the only synagogue in the country that's only 48 percent Jewish. There's an informal Catholic Wives' Club. I'm already on a committee and half are not

Jewish. If we want to rent the parish house for a large gathering, we laugh at remarks such as, "Oh, I'll ask Father Ahearn about that, he baptized me." All of this makes it easy for me to ask Doug how he feels about my ardor for non-Jewish religious music, such as Bach's *Mass in B-Minor* and the *St. Matthew Passion,* and Handel's *Messiah.* "What's the problem?" he answers. "You love the magnificent music because it is written with belief and fervor, and because you have a passion for inspired artistry." I'll buy that.

At Saturday service, Doug's sermon is about damaging gossip, *Lashon Hara,* and he relates the legend about a shtetl where hateful speech flowed like water. The rabbi assembled the townspeople and took a feather pillow in his hand and ripped it open and let the wind carry the feathers to the far corners of the fields and into the woods. The rabbi then told the townspeople to go and collect all the feathers. "Impossible," they cried, "how can we gather what has been scattered?" "So too with your words," advised the rabbi. "You cannot gather these feathers, which are like your words, and bring back every one of them."

At Yom Kippur services I read the Jonah story to the congregation. This is a great honor, and I say that I'm not sure why I am asked. (Of course I know why: because of the book by my son and me about our sea voyage.) I explain that I'm terrified by the sea, and that's reason enough for me to be the reader. I'm allowed to give my own small sermon, and I speak of the three horrifying sea events in the Old Testament, after God made the gentler earth appear from the waters. First, of course, the Flood. Because God took away the land, or increased the sea, mankind perished. Then the crossing of the Red or Reed Sea, where by a similar device the army of the Egyptians was engulfed and drowned. Finally, the story of Jonah, who believed that by crossing this fearsome vastness he could escape from God. (There is another use, in Job, that I missed, and it carries forward the Jonah story's sense of the untameable, perhaps even by God. Note also that in Genesis man is given dominion over the earth and the fishes of the sea, but not over the sea itself.) Then I read to the congregation the passage from *Moby-Dick* that ends, "For as this appalling ocean surrounds the verdant land, so in the soul of man there lies one insular Tahiti, full of peace and joy, but encompassed by all the horrors of the half-known life. God keep thee! Push not off from that isle, thou canst never return!"

The story of Jonah is strange indeed, like an Arabian Nights' tale. We read it on this day of atonement as evidence of God's great forgiveness. But Jonah does not forgive God! Much has been written, as we say.

Back in midweek class, progress is slow. When Jami has trouble concentrating, the power of her mood slows all of us. We practice words appropriate to this time of year, words describing making one's life better: kindness, charity, patience. Doug's story today is about Abraham. I later volunteer that if we have class officers, I'll be the bouncer, explaining that I'm old but crafty and won't fight fair. Doug again says that I will see an enormous change, and patience is okay.

Sunday classes begin with activity in our tiny classroom, but soon we have our full-school assembly. Doug sometimes wears tefillin, and the leather straps wrapped around his muscular arm make him look like a gladiator. How apt as he faces this group. Doug moves constantly, sometimes like a boxer, in a slight but distinct version of in-and-out, feint-and-jab. Sometimes it is more like that bobbing movement of Jewish prayer, which is called *shuckling* and has several explanations, all charming and unsatisfactory. One is that there were too few texts and Jews praying in groups would sway over to get a glimpse of the next passage. Another explanation, by my friend Joanne Greenberg, is that in case you say something wrong it's best to be a moving target. Our services often begin, after an opening prayer, with a request by Doug for news. "We're undefeated in soccer, Rabbi Doug." "Good! Have you played any games?" "Our cat was run over. Are there animals in heaven?" "What do you think?" "If it's a perfect place they have to be there." My child-mind agrees. Animals are a pipeline to perfection, in the heavenly sense, are they not? They are each, in their own way, more perfect children of the creator than we are. As a child I imagined that if we did go up to the Pearly Gates for judgment, our pets would be the judges.

Today, Doug leads a song: "Good Queen Esther went to town, / Bought a kreplach nice and brown / Bit off the corner, then she cried, / 'Goody, goody, goody there's————inside.'" The kids shout out things that could be inside, and we repeat the song many times to accommodate everything from "candy bars" to "toxic waste." Our school, obviously, is not portrayed in the solemn dark etchings you've seen of yeshiva *bochers* (schoolboys) with sad huge eyes and side curls, attended by grave and long-bearded teachers.

In a more serious mood, Doug talks about this day of *t'shuva*, of repentance, of improving our lives by kindness and forgiveness, and we each write a note and seal it in an envelope: we will forgive, we will apologize, we will behave better toward certain persons. We tape the envelope to a plastic copy of a few stones of the Wailing Wall, drastically reduced in size.

I'm making progress. Most of the time I open the book the correct way, which is backward to most of us.

I have continued my private catch-up lessons with Doug, and I do well enough. Doug's explanations are again forgiving. I am encouraged by "That will become clear, don't worry about that," and flattered by "Good question—we're not sure why that is." Then some history, and a new textbook to read on history and customs. Doug explains the Orthodox position that the Torah, the first five books of the Old Testament, our law and the center of Jewish belief, was dictated to Moses during the forty days he spent with God on Mount Sinai. This is a Jewish fundamentalism. In the nineteenth century, Julius Wellhausen, an influential scholar but an anti-Semite, suggested that the Torah was the work of men. Is there a similar situation in Christianity? I ask. "Interesting question." To Doug, all questions are interesting because all people are interesting. "I'm taking divinity courses at Yale. There has been a discussion about this. Many Christians who hold to Wellhausen's view are less inclined to assign the same conclusion to the New Testament." Doug's own view is a compromise that appeals to me: "I believe that God wrote the Torah, but through different people at different times."

Our class on this Sunday is suddenly calm and works well. I mention this to Doug on Tuesday, and he asks, "Who was missing?" I could be excused from class to go to the synagogue building committee meeting, but I choose school instead, and JoAnn Price, our principal, is pleased. Anyway, I don't want to be on the building committee. I should be, because much of my professional work has been designing theaters, similarly dramatic places of assembly. Jewish committees tend to be argumentative, and I've had enough of that in my life. The joke goes this way: the students of a yeshiva, in this case a small Jewish college, want a varsity sport. Which one? They are not numerous enough to have football or baseball squads, and not tall enough for basketball. A suggestion is made that a shell could be borrowed and they could try rowing. This is done, and after a few months they are all rowing in the same direction and with some force, and at the same time the boat stays upright. But before entering intercollegiate competition they want to compare themselves to other teams, so they take the shell to Cambridge and launch it on the Charles and climb in. When the Harvard crew rows by, they set out in pursuit. That night they arrive back at the yeshiva, and the rabbi asks, "How did you do?" "Well, we didn't catch up, but we learned something." "And that was what?" "In the Harvard boat, only one man was yelling."

In class we read some selections from Anne Frank. We must write essays. Should I write about her? Sara says that important physical changes took place in Anne that she'd "rather not talk about." Well, she brought it up, no one else did, and just to get in the old dig, "So much for *you,* stupid boys." Some things have not changed since my hormones sprinted from the gate.

Our teacher, today respectfully addressed as Mrs. Trautmann, leaves the room to get our midmorning tray of cookies and cranberry soda in paper cups. She tells us to read on, but the talk turns instantly to recoloring one's eyes with contact lenses.

A good start today, but whatever heavy sedatives were injected into these kids finally wear off, and Debbie sits outside with Jami for a while. Then we play a game. Debbie has written down facts about Jewish ceremonies on cards. We see them briefly, they are taken away, and then we answer questions. I'm slow to grasp the rules. I'm also slow to memorize, say, the three reasons why white is worn on Yom Kippur. But many of the cards tell a brief story or legend, and these I can repeat almost perfectly after a swift glance. At that I'm the best! Then we get a new book, a dictionary. I'm pleased to get a new textbook.

Only a week after Yom Kippur it is Sukkot, a holiday week cel-
ebrating the years of wandering in the desert and the gifts of nature that sustained us. A tentlike structure, the sukkah, is built and
decorated to suggest the harvest. Part of it must be open to the sky.
A meal under the tent or lattice is a treat, and our workbook tells
us that some traditional Jews live, eat and sleep in their sukkah for
the entire eight days of the festival, in keeping with the verse in
Leviticus 24, commanding every citizen of Israel to dwell in the
sukkah.

In class we pass the *tzedakah* (charity) box. One of the greatest
mitzvahs is giving to charity. We're starting the lifelong habit.
Aaron passes me a piece of gum. We discuss freedom and decide
that it's to do what you want—but with laws. Jami asks why are we
talking about this? Why aren't we doing the lesson we prepared?
Good move, Jami. My guess is that she hasn't prepared.

We're to go on a field trip. I'm the only student without a per-
mission slip from home. We go into the youngest group's classroom and choose a partner. I choose Matthew, who tells me he's
seven.

We make birds, each bird representing the soul of a dead
friend or relative, an Iranian custom. We punch pinholes in eggs.
Matthew patiently blows out the white and yolk. I break mine and
am given a second. I make a slightly larger hole and suck out the
egg, which is easier than blowing. I hide this, because I don't want
a lot of *Yecchs!* from the class or, worse, have it thought that the
new kid (me) is showing off. Raw egg is a taste acquired from
gulping those pick-me-ups that dancers and other show folk
called "Martha Graham Specials." (In a glass we beat up a raw egg
or two, then added sugar, Tiger's Milk or wheat germ, and perhaps
some real milk.)

We cut out wings, beaks, and tails from sheets of colored paper and glue them to the eggs. I design an efficient wing-and-tail assembly with a built-in hole for the string, and Matthew cuts it out carefully with blunt scissors. But the other kids' wings, less sophisticated, look better.

There is a brief recess. My classmates always know where to go. They hang together and dart and wheel through the hallways like a flock of pigeons. They've been together for over five years. I stumble about, looking for the men's room.

We get on a school bus. This is the first time in my privileged life that I've been on a yellow school bus. I'm told that the best seats are in the back because it's bumpier, and indeed our most aggressive kids are carrying on there, mostly in midair. I sit with Matthew, who is quiet.

It's almost two miles from the annex to the synagogue, our destination. We walk across the street toward it. Matthew puts his warm little hand in mine. My heart jumps! Trust? Affection? Just habit, crossing the street? All or any will do. We hang our bird from the lattice that forms the roof of the little sukkah that has been put up on the synagogue lawn. Matthew points to exactly where he wants it. He laboriously knots a string around the carrot he's brought, and I hang that beside the bird. We go inside the synagogue. He reads the prayers easily, in Hebrew, or maybe he's reading the transliteration under the Hebrew. Smart kid.

The autumn colors are dazzling. On the ride back to the annex, Matthew leans against me. He says, "Look, I've lost a tooth!" Big gappy smile. At school I drive away as he waits to be picked up by his parents.

Chapter 6

☆ ☆ ☆

THE NEW HOUSE AT THE TOP OF THE DRIVEWAY

MY DAUGHTER, JULIA, is what we call "organized." She's run this family since she learned to read at six and could order Chinese takeout. She became my fund-raiser for The National Theatre of the Deaf and tripled the gifts in a few months. Those were delicious years. She would come to this town three days a week, and we would work in the same office, and she would stay in our tiny old house here. What father doesn't enjoy setting up housekeeping with his daughter?

Now she has three little boys. The last, sunny, delightful Jed, was intended to be a girl, but even a boy can be a keeper, and the moment of disappointment at the results of the amnio-something passed quickly.

Leonora said, "Cheer up, maybe he'll be gay."

When Julia can't arrange for a baby-sitter or parental escort for football, soccer, hockey, lacrosse, basketball, piano lessons, Hebrew school, tennis lessons, or just play dates, she knows six weeks in advance and drafts grandparents. This morning I'm taking eight-year-old Jesse for his baseball team photo. He's been grounded, basically for being eight, and will miss the first game, but you can't keep him off the team for the whole season. He's paroled for the photo, then straight home and inside. In the afternoon it's Jordan's turn. He's six, and this is his first year in the league. His uniform, a tee shirt extending down to his knees, is a gorgeous lime green announcing THE GREEN HORNETS. The coach is attentive and effective in batting practice as the youngsters hit the ball off the tee. Then they race over to the photographer. The coach suddenly becomes stupid, mystified at the paperwork, and I help. The team photo is free, but the profit for the photographer is in the extras: a dozen trading cards or a sports magazine cover featuring the little slugger in full color. I heard the photographer's spiel earlier. It's ordinary, but it works. "Watch closely as I roll up my sleeves, my hands will never leave my arms!" Each child is hauled to the plate, given a bat, and told to face the camera. Almost half are girls. The faces! The uncertainty, the vulnerability, the professional glitz of the uniform, a carapace to a child who doesn't know exactly where to face or how to look. That's the photo! Doesn't the photographer see it? Why should he? It's his two-hundredth child today. He just wants to make sure that the coach, who is now racing with the wind after the sign-up sheets that he dropped, brings them back in the right order. And he does want to make a living. But the faces! Why not a before-and-after? All the gold anyone could dream of is in those glorious insecure faces. One by one they are spoiled, transformed into lifeless income by the touch of this Midas of the lens. "Face this way. Lift your chin. Turn your shoulder." Then, when the imitation of a million-dollar sportsman can go no further, "Pizza!" The smile, the flash. "Great shot! Next!"

. A week later I drive down for the school play. Jordan plays a monkey and recites his lines perfectly. "If you cut down the tree, when the rains come the roots will not hold the soil and the forest will become a desert." Julia has made the monkey costumes, black sweatpants to which she has sewn stiff twelve-inch tails. My own concern is that Jordan, who has a deep sense of humor that bubbles up, will put the pants on backward. The masks, fierce and colorful and mysterious, are of rain-forest animals and rid most of the children of shyness. Things go as well and as audibly as can be expected, and the weak point always, the principal's curtain speech, is witty enough and almost short enough. We forbid curtain speeches in our Little Theatre of the Deaf, which tours in schools. We've had too many performances chilled by, "These special people are so wonderful that you're going to love them and then you're all going to write letters to them." Or, just before our opener, in which we teach a few sign language words, "Now be good children and sit on your hands."

That night we go to a dinner at Julia and Jack's synagogue, a converted home. Jack grew up immersed in Jewish tradition: candles and blessings on the Sabbath eve, holidays, the foods, bar and bat mitzvah. His mother, Marsha, had earned her living as a musician in the Catskills. Devout? Not a bit. Cultural? Totally. When they found the house they wanted, in the suburbs near New York City, Julia phoned about the schools, Jack about the Jewish community. Julia's entrance into the community was immediate and consuming: the PTO, a library-fund drive, getting the children to activities. Jack entered through the congregation, first as a board member and then as president.

Tables are set in the main room of the synagogue, and after the briefest of services, the men are asked to go into the kitchen to wash hands. It's steamy and full of women moving swiftly and precisely, finishing the platters of food, wiping their sweaty foreheads with their forearms, an image from an Italian postwar film. We wash. The ritual here is to pour water from a small mug onto one hand and then onto the other. We eat. The dining room is crowded. Jed is now walking and smiling, out of sight under the table rims. One can see his progress by the adult, Julia or Jack or Leonora, who walks slowly behind him like a barrage balloon. My favorite comment on this little boy is Julia's: "When I go to get him in the morning, he's often turned away from me in the crib, and when I come near I see the side of his face wrinkle in a smile."

I like these people. If I don't really like one of them or if someone is angry at me, I know how to state my case or defend myself. Family, for better or worse.

Daniel's infrequent trips East are high moments for his nephews. Suddenly they learn so much about themselves and each other. Recently I came into their room after lights out. Dan was asleep on his chosen firm mattress of floor, between the beds. Jesse lay next to him in his sleeping bag, still awake, the scoundrel, listening to the Knicks game on headphones. Jordan was asleep in his unique gravity-defying style, head thrown back, somehow staying on his bed with more than half of him cantilevered out into space.

"Jess," I whispered, "you're lying next to one of the greatest guys that ever lived."

"No, Poppa, next to the *two* greatest guys that ever lived."

Two days before Dan had tooled into Pelham in his pridefully filthy pickup with its bullet holes, winches, and wired-on exhaust pipes, everything a wilderness guide needs to enrapture Jesse, Jordan and the adolescent-at-heart of all ages. The three males were so quiet for so long in the backyard that Julia finally walked out to see the action. There they stood, in silent awe, as Dan's truck swayed gently, suspended by its winch cable from a tree limb.

On Sunday, Jordan and I drive up to the marine museum in South Norwalk, shouting out the alphabet letters we see along I-95. We eat at McDonald's, wander through the tentative exhibits, see a space film on a huge screen, and then drive to the north end of town to see my old home. We had moved in during the summer of 1941, when I was eleven. Forty-three years later, my daughter and her cousin Laurie had to plead with my mother and then lead her from the emptied house where she'd lived alone for twenty-four years after my father died. "My sunsets," she said.

The property was beautiful, and a menthol-cigarette company had photographed the misty cool-looking waterfall and reproduced it on the sides of their trucks, forty feet long. When Mom saw one of these, she would dart through traffic and rap on the cab door. "That's my waterfall!" she would cry up to the astonished driver.

There had been a wooded plot along the road, but there is a house there now, sharing the first twenty yards of the old driveway. We drive down past it to the parking area between the front of the old house and the waterfall. We get out and I hold Jordan's hand. I'd been back once to pick up some things we'd forgotten and had been welcomed by the new owners but staggered by what they had done in the large living room. Mom's American antiques and muted colors were replaced by Spanish ironwork furniture in red and gold, a display that would have set the teeth of the madams in Rome who greeted me when I was a student.

The waterfall has also changed; boulders have tumbled up against the dam and shortened the fall of water. "Over there, Jordan, there were woods, and *my* dad made beautiful paths among them. We had a bridge over the river—there—just long logs with planks between. You could walk way to the back, where all of those houses are now, and then walk across another bridge and to the tip of that island, where it's just messy and overgrown now . . .

"Here's where we used to swim, Jordan. And we walked along the top of the waterfall. And we put on our skates here. Once we made a diving helmet—I'll draw it for you later—and we pumped air to it through a garden hose with a bicycle pump, and we could walk along the bottom of the pond, right around that bend." Jordan is only mildly interested. How long can you stand with a little boy and tell him that what he sees wasn't there, and what was there can't be seen anymore. "When your mother was just your age, we used to climb on the rocks here or hold on to a rope in the swift part. And we swung out from a tree and dropped into the pond from that—Well, there used to be a tree there. Come on, let's get an ice-cream soda." "What's an ice-cream soda, Poppa?" Can he imagine his mother as a six-year-old, his age, a platinum-blond girl yelling and laughing as the water tumbled her over?

The pond, my old world. Not just light separated from darkness or the waters separated from dry land. This was the layered half-world of shadow between light sky and dark earth, water and bottom ooze, half water, half earth, something not mentioned in the creation, something that has grown and mouldered since Genesis. We glided in it in our homemade diving helmet or in our masks and goggles, adventurers and explorers. We struggled ashore through waist-deep rotting leaves like amphibians slithering up to dry land. We tipped the painted turtles off the lily pads and raced them to the bottom. We hovered in the depths in moonlight, our shadows dancing below. We watched the progress of snapping turtles working their way upstream in the river, mud-colored turtles as big around as your arms could circle. The ducks came from the sky to rest on the middle world, the surface of the pond, and once I saw three ducklings pulled down from that stillness, one after the other, down into the mud. When a sharp freeze iced the river in one night—black ice we called it—we could glide on our skates a half-mile upstream, like long-legged beetles on the unwrinkled crystal, suspended over the clear and winter-swept bottom.

"Hello there! David, is that really you?" On our way up the driveway there is a burst of sound with the sunshine. "This is my house!" The woman's voice is from the house at the top of the driveway, the house that straddles the steep slide down into the pond, covering the spot where we launched our sleds, to be airborne halfway down and then to hit bottom with a crunch and rocket out across the ice. In astonishment, I answer. "Is that you, your house? I knew you'd moved here, but *here?*"

"Come in for milk and cookies."

We do that, and sit with a handsome gracious woman in an airy house filled with the pictures and furniture of her mother, Mary Martin, a blazing star in all of our lives for the same forty years that we had lived down the driveway. I'd seen her when I was a teenager, and adored her of course, and who could have believed that forty-five years later I'd be sitting holding hands with the frail dying lady in a California garden, looking at mountains and talking about flying, not airplanes, not even Peter Pan suspension onstage, just personal flying, the easy kind, just rising, floating and gliding away.

The Theatre of the Deaf performs that little Haiku poem: "Carrying mother on my back, just for a lark / Suddenly weeping, she's so light!"

Another, younger lady, the granddaughter of the star, joins us.

I describe our life here as it had been: the pond, the fish, the turtles, where the hockey goals were put on the ice. We can see most of it from this deck, the view is the same as it was from a tree house I'd built just here fifty-five years ago. The pond needs dredging, and the places where we could step ashore from the canoe are overgrown. They only needed a snip or two by my father every morning on his walk before he went in to the city. Perhaps the condominium committee hasn't decided who's in charge. For this woman, here now with her family, the view is fresh and beautiful, and the houses across the river seem well designed, all with large windows facing the pond, and perhaps many children thrash around and laugh in the water and mud, not just the rich kids and their few selected friends.

A double sycamore rises majestically between the pond and our old house. In front of the dining room, which was on the second floor, a slim branch shot out and scattered foreground green against the waterfall. A Japanese touch, the precious and unexpected breath-catching note of beauty. *Shibui,* they say. One year the Davey tree men, with casual indifference, lopped off this branch. My mother shouted and then wept, real tears, and the man said, "Lady, it'll grow back." "Yes," said Mom, "it will grow back, it will, but not in my lifetime."

It is growing back. Almost three feet in the fifteen years, six feet to go, possibly only ten years more if it speeds up. Could that have been the real start of Mom's last journey, was that the moment of the distant sound, the string breaking in the air, the moment she knew that her time had come to step down from her house and her sunsets?

Jordan gravely sips his ginger ale while we adults talk of the star, of how we miss her, of how generations pass. Too much old-time stuff for Jordan. We walk to the car. "Poppa, I'm going to love you even when you're dead." "Sure you will, and if you remember all the fun and laughing we do, I'll still be a part of you, and not dead." I grab his hand, we walk a few steps. "Gimme your hand, Jordan." "Poppa, it's already there." He falls asleep almost instantly, next to me on the front seat.

From our prayer book: "In the rising of the sun and its going down, we remember them. . . . In the opening of buds . . . in the blueness of the sky . . . in the rustling of leaves and the beauty of autumn, we remember them. . . . So long as we live, they too shall live."

Chapter 7

✶   ✶   ✶

COLUMBUS SAYS SHALOM

OUG'S STORIES ARE captivating. Imagine growing up with a grandmother who refuses to mention age. The mal-angels will hear and snatch you, even if you're just a kid and your one-figure age is mentioned at your own birthday party. And, as the brilliant Yiddishist Michael Wex tells us, don't think those angels perched and waiting on your shoulders are stupid; they're Jewish too. One way Doug's grandmother might state it, and try this for precision: "She's 65–120." Somewhere between is the meaning. One hundred and twenty was Moses' age at death, and it has become the mythic finish line for a long life. Doug—who else?—sets up the chairs at the synagogue before services, and it's fun, he says, he remembers putting boxes in order at his grandfather's grocery near Boston. His great-grandfather was a shammes—a synagogue janitor—in Minsk, so he comes from a long line of janitors. Leonora comes from a short line of janitors who never mastered the work. Before coming to this country, her grandfather was advised to send all of the family money to a brother-in-law who would invest it, because the streets here were paved with gold. This was done and the money was lost, and not repaid when the brother-in-law became wealthy again. So the family, "Practically royalty in Hungary," whatever that means, ended up taking out the garbage in a Harlem tenement. There my beloved wife spent her early years, supported in infancy by her Aunt Clara, the most practical of the four sisters ("The Poor Man's Gabors," to quote one of many husbands). Clara was a manicurist and had boyfriends. Figure it out. Then Leonora's mother sent her to a superb public school, P.S.6, by the simple device of falsifying her address. This was easy because of the baroque gerrymandering of that school district, intricately engineered by the rich to exclude the poor, and so confusing that the rich couldn't keep track of it. Then came scholarships and then, at fourteen, the child was earning her own living as a dancer under faked working papers. Then she was enrolled in three colleges at once, and this taught her how to keep track, to prioritize the important things, which does not include her own age, lost in the confusion of various forged birth certificates. She is now 60–120.

Doug is so encouraging! You can't do anything wrong! Of course from time to time you can *improve* what may not be perfect.

"Doug, this language isn't as easy as it was when you said it was easy." Doug: "THAT'S RIGHT! It's not an easy language."

I'm comfortable in class. I now see Rachel as a friend, through my new twelve-year-old eyes. It has taken time because of her quietness, not from any lack of warmth. She is an adopted child, born in Guatemala. She is dark skinned with glossy black hair and the serene beauty of the great Aztec heads. One can't avoid visualizing the sexist, even racist vision of this young lady in a sarong. Already, at her age, it wouldn't slip down. She is the intense personification of the change, of the growing sexuality, of these kids. She is impassive in class and never volunteers or interrupts or shows a need to let off steam. She is always prepared and ready to recite or participate. She is, Doug confides, sprightly and luminous at her home. Doug goes there and all over. He is coaching each of these youngsters in their homes, once a week, to prepare them for bar or bas mitzvah. Some live almost thirty minutes away.

Now, in October, we are joined by Hannah, who is pretty and small and quiet. She's come up from the class below, her birthday places her between the classes. She has a light voice and is not aggressive. She never interrupts the class and, like Rachel, is always prepared. She has an aura of keen observation about her, an artist-to-be in some discipline. She shines when we play word games.

By now I'm doing well enough in my Hebrew; the back of the class is in sight ahead. I know my letters, but the promised twenty-two have different forms, particularly when they end a word. Those dots and dashes that make up the five vowels ("EASY!") appear in different places, and often I have trouble finding them. Then there are those letters that have no sound at all, but are still with us because they once were with us, or because you need something over or under which to place the dots and dashes of the vowels. But I'm getting past some confusions and relaxing a bit, knowing that the learning of new skills doesn't proceed smoothly but jumps up from plateau to plateau. That's the way the tide comes in, did you ever notice? The rise is not steady but will pause, then lift quickly on a tiny tidal wave, almost imperceptible in most places. Then it will pause again. I hear again my own advice and words of comfort to my many students over the years. Soon, I know, my tide in this language will be high enough so that words will form for me at a glance. Already I can see as a group the Hebrew letters that form great words—*"Baruch Atah Adonai,"* and simple words are starting to jump out at me, like "shalom" and "Israel," not to mention "amen," which we pronounce "Amein."

Like most kids in these classes I will learn the meaning of each prayer and of key words and be able to read phonetically, but grammar and word-for-word translation skills are another matter. At Friday evening services I can now read along phonetically, but so many of the words in the prayer book contain one big fat letter that I'm convinced I've never seen before, and I stumble. How interesting it is to learn a language at this age. It's not hard to imagine being a man who's had a stroke, and to whom the English alphabet gives no clues: he has to learn to read all over again. I have friends who've experienced this, and I'm getting to that risky age myself.

Sunday we have a guest speaker who is the synagogue's fundraiser and a scholar. Appropriately, the subject is the upcoming Columbus Day. What does this have to do with Jews? Plenty, says our speaker. He tells of the 1492 Inquisition in Spain. His most charming story is about why Jews don't point at stars. He knew this, but not why, and one night his fiancée pointed at stars, and he said *"Don't do that!"* Years later he found out why. The inquisitors would wait on Saturday evenings outside houses of Jews who claimed to have converted. If people came out of a house and pointed to the stars—because they needed to see three stars before the Sabbath was declared over—they must still be Jews!

Instrumental in financing the first voyage of Columbus, he tells us, was an ex-Jew named Luis de Santangel not, as the children's myth would have it, Isabella selling her jewels. The second voyage, he says, was financed by the money Jews were forced to leave behind when they fled Spain in 1492.

The great map makers of the time were Jewish, and the perfecter of the astrolabe was Jewish. At that time, there were 1,000,000 Jews in the world, 600,000 in Spain.

Luis de Torres, Columbus' translator, was also an ex-Jew, or Marrano. He had been a translator in Spain, and Hebrew was his specialty. When the Jews were exiled, there was no one left who needed his work, so he went to sea. Our speaker's point is that he was first ashore in the New World, so it's more than likely that the first European word spoken here was "Shalom." Maybe Columbus said it also! What a good idea. Then our smiling speaker adds that when Columbus took possession in the name of Spain, he probably stated, in the fashion of that year, "And no Jew shall be allowed here." He also tells us that the first governor of Cuba was a Jew. Cortés had ex-Jews with him, and many settled in the southwest of what is now the United States, and lately we have realized that some Jewish rituals are blended into Native American customs. My own reading informs me that there is much circumstantial evidence that Columbus had Jewish members in his family tree.

We learn that Jews came to New Amsterdam from Brazil and were refused entry, but they presented a letter from the Dutch East India Company. This was accepted, and they stayed and established the first synagogue, in 1654. Emma Lazarus, who wrote the poem inscribed on the Statue of Liberty, descended from those Jews.

Sunday we start the assembly with a portion of the prayer service. Then three of the children give Doug objects, and he has fifteen seconds to make a sermon from them. The objects are a jar of syrup, an empty bottle and a small piece of paper on which is written "I can, I will." Doug begins: "In life, sometimes you feel that there are things you want to do but just can't. You'll get into a *sticky situation*. But you must say '*I can, I will*,' or else you'll end up—*empty*."

"Hey," shouts a chubby boy of about eleven, "you said the sermon has to be about Judaism!"

"Okay," says Doug, "try this." "At your bar mitzvah, are you afraid that the words will *stick* in your throat?"

We go to class, and Doug tells us that on November 1st we will lead the Friday evening services. There is lively dispute about who will say what section. Adam simply refuses but will relent, I'm sure. Jami doesn't refuse. I don't say a word. We read some of the prayers, Aaron slowly, Jami swiftly, and I am transported back to my third-grade classroom, where we had about the same reading level in English that we have here in Hebrew. Not bad! But I recall my fast reading, as fast as the girls, except one, and I remember two of my old classmates still picking their way, as I do now, word by word. Afterward I ask Doug about the particularly hard prayer that I've been sounding out, The *V'ahavta*. This is the prayer that instructs us to love our God. Yes, Doug agrees, that's a tough one, lots of double-sounding consonants. I'm encouraged because I can almost do it.

We are all present in class. We read about the bar/bas mitzvah process in our workbook. Preparation is a big responsibility. Mastery will give us a sense of achievement, the ceremony a sense of accomplishment. We will, after bar mitzvah, have a sense of our strengths and weaknesses, and a chance to receive more responsibilities. Sara stars in the discussion and talks about being frightened that she'll not be a good mother. She has a diary and writes down her troubles. She has invented a cartoon figure, and when the troubles are all written down and said by that character, she sometimes throws away the drawing and text. This is like the legend (not accurate but amusing) of the goat that escapes (or is banished or sacrificed), carrying (tied to his horns?) a message of our troubles and iniquities—yes, the escape-goat.

Mark's main concern at this moment is that the high school he will attend may not have good computers. After class, he offers to help me learn to use my word processor.

I always want to say more, but my few attempts have been ponderous and lengthy. Debbie is right to keep us moving. The next workbook question: what we will lose as we age? Sara says our innocence. What does she really mean? I say that we may lose our imaginations, and that's not understood. Later I ask Sara what she means by innocence, and she is clear that she doesn't mean sexual innocence, but that the ceremony, while it won't make a sudden change, will gently close the door on childhood.

We go to Aleph, the first grade, to help them perform a dramatized version of the creation. Doreen Joslow reads. She is a woman of enormous energy who married a Jew and, wanting to learn more about the religion, is teaching the youngest class. I play piccolo accompaniment and apologize later to Doug for falling into so many versions of "Amazing Grace." "That's okay," he says. "We'll have to put our own lyrics to it." In our play, Sara becomes God and Mark volunteers to be the defense attorney of the twenty-two letters of the Hebrew alphabet. They will appear before God and argue that they can do whatever She needs. The kids become animals and stars and angels as the reading progresses. After, I suggest to Mark that the defense attorney should check his yo-yo with the bailiff before summing up.

Little Matthew is in the Aleph group. He doesn't recognize me.

We have a tallit lesson with Doug before the service. He shows us how to kiss the embroidered center edge of the prayer shawl and then swing it like a cape onto our shoulders. The center edge shows up on the back of your neck. The seat next to me is always the last taken. I overhear small triumphs of the younger kids: "You're lucky, your bookmark ribbon is longer than mine." Doug asks for personal news. A girl has been cast in *The Wizard of Oz*. One boy is getting a dog.

Prayer books have a soul, Doug was taught, so treat them respectfully. Doug refers often to his teachers of his own bar mitzvah, his teachers in high school (New Jersey), and finally in "rabbi school," and he does this with enthusiasm and respect. Doug's reverence for his masters is understood by these bright youngsters and means to them that just as Doug learned from his teachers, they too can learn.

Then we do ART. We make moiré book-cover papers by dipping paper into blobs of oil paint that are floating on water. Mark tells me that I'm a seventeen-year-old in a white wig. He calls me Dave. Loathsome nickname; it's not me and I hate it. But kids don't control their names, and if that's the drill, I can't object.

The next Tuesday, with Doug, I open my Torah portion. Not the real Torah, but a copy of my portion in the bar mitzvah preparation pamphlet. The Torah lettering is strange to me, more ornamented, more blocky, without vowels and cantillation marks. It wasn't until about 700 C.E. (Common Era, our preference to A.D.) that the Masoretes (scribes) started writing the vowels and musical notes and punctuation marks, but the Torah itself did not change.

I am thrilled, I'm becoming a part of the tradition, the mysteries. This is the Law, in ancient letters, the great twenty-two. It is in front of me, there is one paragraph of it that I can sing.

Doug tells me that there are powerful fundamentalists in Israel who resist any language change. Our language is not ordinary because God wrote it Himself, as the belief goes. There recently lived in Israel a man who tried to expand these symbols, and his house is still frequently vandalized, and the memorial plaque torn off. I've been told elsewhere that the great stories of Sholom Aleichem are not easy to translate from Yiddish into Hebrew. The Hebrew we are reading is the Hebrew of the Law and prayers and commentaries. Recently it has become used by more people and for everyday purposes, in Israel, but it has yet to grow fully in this direction and does not possess the variety of slang and idioms that these stories require.

On November 17th we talk about who we are. I say I'm changing and don't know, and that's why I'm here. Mark, going for the dramatic effect, says that his mother is an Irish Catholic and his father is a Jew and he was given the choice and boy did he make the wrong one. Then we're given a sizable piece of blank paper and the crayons are brought out and we're asked to draw what Judaism means to us at this holiday season. The kids start right in, noses to paper, drawing like mad. Menorahs and that sort of thing appear. Mark does a patchwork and it's a fine symbol of the interlocking things we are studying. I stare at my blank sheet and icy sweat runs down my back. I'm sure that Debbie wouldn't have given me this assignment if she knew of my years of deadlines and the anguish that a blank piece of paper brings back to me. In London I was apprenticed to Leslie Hurry, a marvelous painter and designer and a genuine and delightful crazyman, and one of my jobs was to take a new pad of drawing or watercolor paper and scribble lightly in it or soil or wrinkle each page so that he never had to face a crisp virgin sheet. He needed paper that had character, a tilt or an attitude or at least a cordial informality so that he could *transform* it, as opposed to creating on it from zilch. Now I sit alone, gazing at the paper. The kids are done and out of the room. Can't I do some other deed? Clean toilets? I ask Debbie if I can be excused from this assignment. I've spent my life creating on blank sheets, I've shown reasonable commitment, can she forgive this cowardice? Yes, I am excused.

I do not dodge all assignments. When we are asked to write our own version of the Ten Commandments, I reduce them to three. First, the usual rule, do unto others, etc. There is a lovely story about this. The great Hillel was asked (under the threat of death, the legend states) to recite the entire Torah while standing on one leg. He lifted a foot and said, "Do unto others as you would have them do to you," and then he stood on both feet again. "All the rest," he said, "is commentary." It is said that after Hillel's comment about commentary, he added, "Go learn," which gives greater stature indeed to the "commentary." Of course there is disagreement here. He probably said, "Do not do unto others that which is hateful to yourself." This kind of distinction between a supposed Jewish version and a more aggressive, proselytizing Christian version has, of course, been the subject of much discussion.

My second commandment is the BR, the Big Rule, and Dan and I developed it to get us over sticky spots during our long voyage together. It goes: "If you're going to laugh about it in six months or a year, you might as well start laughing now; it saves time." It's a good rule. Doug tells me that he's trying to adopt it himself. My third commandment is "Sing more." I draw these instructions on my paper in two circles, the rims of spectacles, as if you must look through these glasses to see everything. Then I'm pleased that my teacher tacks this crayon drawing to the wall. It's really one of the best! After the school year I'll take it home and stick it on the refrigerator door.

Chapter 8

☆   ☆   ☆

FALLING APART

M Y IMAGES ARE nourishing and usually in Technicolor, detailed because of my visual training. Some are images of sound only, and these can be powerful at night. Some combine sound and sight, or even the presence of a strong silence, as in my image of a ballet I designed for Balanchine. Glorious accidents (not totally accidental) created a stage quality so enchanting that when the curtain fell the audience was transfixed and could not applaud. This is never a flash image: it lasts and lasts until that first tentative applause shatters it.

At night my image is often Cape Horn, I see the light of a cloud-etched moonbeam through a porthole that I made, and the oval swings across the ceiling. I hear a voice, not my father's voice, which spoke to me for so long after he died but is now being succeeded, in this moment, by the voice of my son: "Dad, I think I see The Horn."

In New York City I designed plays and musicals, operas and

ballets, then I started The National Theatre of the Deaf, and my remembered scenes are rich. In 1969, I stand yelling at an airplane
pilot, and he is yelling back, and I will not give him a waiver of lia-
bility from this company of deaf actors who may not hear his
instructions. He *will* carry this troupe to Europe, as fully enfran-
chised people. They know what to do in emergencies. And he did
carry them, furious at me. The takeoff seemed abrupt.

Framed images, nourishing but lonely as they hang fixed and
completed on the gallery walls of memory. Here I can see the Roman amphitheatre at Caesaria, in Israel, where we dressed in the
dirt-floored catacombs, where we saw a full moon rising over the
steep curve of seating holding two thousand people, packed in.
Then their ovation. Survivors from Europe, gone now most of
them, who understood that what was happening on stage was the
reason for our civilization, not an embellishment to it.

As vivid, but on a smaller canvas: a skinny little girl, no more
than seven, dressed immaculately in white tights, patent-leather
pumps, a brilliant red-velvet dress, her hair done in a thousand
tiny, glossy braids with yellow ribbons. She is sitting on the edge,
the very edge of her chair, watching our Little Theatre perform at
Lincoln Center, leaning out to the actors.

A final picture for now, the most powerful for me of a lifetime
of memories of curtains up and curtains down. We are in a city in
Japan. At the curtain call there is a standing ovation. A dozen ten-
year-old girls run down the two aisles and climb to the stage by
stairs on either side. To these magical actors each presents a full
bouquet of flowers. The girls bow, the actors from America bow,
their arms full of flowers. The city is Hiroshima.

One of those young actors was a man I'll call Ravenal. Three
weeks ago, as I write this, he was sentenced to a year in prison for

theft and embezzlement from that company of actors that I began and that I loved.

Is this crime another reason that has placed me in a tiny schoolroom with a teacher and eight twelve-year-olds, wondering if the girl sitting next to me knows that her nail polish is green, with gold stars? Am I pursuing this study because of the Curse and the utterance to Doug, the passing but ineradicable mention of that initiation that I missed at thirteen? Or is it because of the milestone of my mother's death? Yes, and here is another reason. It has to do with a miserable chapter in my life. The "pilgrimage gene" dictated to me that I must announce, to God or to no one in particular, "If I get out of this mess, I'll _____" (Fill in this blank. Walk on my knees to Mecca? Take a mime to lunch?) The mess was far worse than hives. Getting out of it became a part of my trip to the bema. It came in a wrapping of evil and adventure and questioning, and I passed, but not with flying colors. It nourished my journey. I thought of it as a fight to recover. Now, in memory, I see that it too is framed and that it is about growing old, about loss.

The theater company that I started was not my idea; that's to the credit of Edna Levine and Mary Switzer, brought to me by Arthur Penn, Anne Bancroft, and Gene Lasko. I put my heart into over thirty years of work with The National Theatre of the Deaf, and it is beautiful theatrically and powerful socially: it has changed hundreds of thousands of lives. I believe that no other American theater company has been to five continents. I believe that no other world theater company has been to six. We've appeared on seven.

I love the dramatic medium of Sign Language with voice. I'm not deaf, and people wonder why I did all that, and I comment that we never had any real hearing problems in my family, just listening problems. Sign Language illuminates and focuses communication, creates the one-at-a-time conversation that is so rare today. But after thirty years I was burned out. Our staff was always small, and when I had a good idea, everyone would look at me and cry "Great! Do it!" When you're exhausted and the only way to save your life is to stop getting ideas, you're burned out. Then the crime, and I was pulled back in and there were few things I wanted less to do.

I sat there doggedly for two years, trying to keep the company alive. I ran out of my cubicle to say "Gesundheit!" when one of our loyal and beloved staff sneezed. I became exhausted, my back to the wall, explaining and defending the delicate balances of our operation. I kept vital contracts from being canceled, I tried to maintain our image and practices as higher than ordinary businesses in the face of businesspeople who were placed, by our lawyers, in charge of the emergency committee. Those I had to deal with were clever but limited, whose instincts were to change talent and ideas, which are something, into money, which is nothing. Our aim had always been to do the opposite. My failure, as I look back, is that with so much defensive skirmishing on the quarterdeck, I lost the chance to trim our work to new winds and set a bold new course.

I began to attend Friday night services at the synagogue. I couldn't follow the Hebrew, but there was plain English as well. I was tired and often I just slept, but if I sat next to a friend I would be tapped on the shoulder when we stood, which was often. The words I enjoyed most in the service were "You may sit." I was soothed and gained perspective in the presence of these friends who all had been through frustration. A congregation indeed. And I loved Doug's sermons. Doug describes sermonizing as being like the tooth fairy: you work while others sleep. But I woke for them.

My need to take the pilgrimage with Rabbi Doug grew on me during these long days. One of our lawyers, a tall man, homely like

Lincoln and deserving of trust, posed the question: "You know, David, that you'll have to forgive 'Ravenal' some day." "Why?" I asked. He then told me a story about a Japanese and an American who had become so enraged with each other that neither had a peaceful night of sleep for many years. Probably a prisoner-of-war story. Finally they met, forgave each other, and were at peace.

I pondered this forgiveness as we collected pennies to meet payroll. But we would be saved, principally by Leonora, who raised $100,000 in the first blush of our emergency, and by Michael Price and his board, from the nearby Goodspeed Opera, who added a loan. This was the bridge, more like a high wire, on which we balanced, not missing an obligation, until we reached relative safety.

After two years I replaced myself, and now I could get started with Doug. Sadly, it was no longer enjoyable to stand back and cheer on the younger people who now ran the company. The chain had snapped. It was too wide a gulf for me, retooling with what we had salvaged, too far from our founding energy and delight. Old age overtook the part of me that was my own life's work, and the change came not as a process but as a sudden discovery. Time, we know, is not a thief but an embezzler. How apt. Suddenly, no longer "this is," but "that was."

But it was spring again, and Leonora's annual cry rang forth, "Look! The carcasses are coming up!"

Chapter 9

* * *

WE SING THE LATKE SONG

I HAVE DREAMS OF my old work. I drift through the carpentry shops, the paint shops, I greet my friends, so many of them dead now. We talk of holes in the masking, where the audience can see us at work backstage. We talk of old Bill ("Bugs") who got so mad that he hung the drops backward, and got madder still when I told him that I wanted the painted side toward the audience. I dream of a long stroll through a prop warehouse, where you could rent anything from a roomful of Chinese Chippendale to an oversize ebony giraffe, made in that ferocious Indian Raj style that looks like a cow pie with a million angry black flies buzzing around it. But judgments are relaxed in these dreams. I wish my old friends well.

In class I find another surprise, another rejuvenation. I loved college, I was of a generation that didn't rebel, that confidently soaked in the old stuff. The huge course catalogue was to me one of the Great Books. After high school, where the only elective choice was between French or Spanish, this book of courses that I could select brought ecstasy to me. I pored over it for days when it arrived in the mail before I went to register, and again for hours each fall and spring. And if you couldn't take the courses, you could audit and enjoy the lectures by stars like John Finley or Arthur Schlesinger. I was swept along in giddy delight for my four years and I excelled. There is a joy in formal scholarship that has been missing. I'd almost forgotten it, and here it is again; my life is changing. I sit with young students in class, exploring the Old Testament with its enigmatic and dysfunctional families, sitting with bright, questioning young people, led by Doug who is always prepared with comments from the rabbis through the centuries and, more exciting, his own.

We discuss our Eternal Flame, which is an electric light in a lanternlike casing suspended over the Ark. Leonora calls it "a hangdown from the past." It is a symbol of the embers that always glowed at the Temple, ready to be stirred into flame for the sacrifices. But I wonder if the Eternal Flame earns its place if it's electric, or even a gas flame, like JFK's memorial. Pale reproduction of a symbol. Isn't vigilance the message here? Cy Taubman, our treasurer, pays the synagogue's electric bill once a month, probably when reminded by his wife. Is that enough? It seems a desecration of the idea to handle it this easily. Maybe Jackie Kennedy Onassis missed the boat on the JFK memorial. A better idea—build a guardhouse by the memorial, just big enough for two cots and a tiny fridge and a burner for cocoa, plus a toilet and an alarm clock. Then invite, for twenty-four hours of vigil, pairs of sixteen-year-olds, *to tend a real fire.* Two youngsters who might be from totally different backgrounds, two young people who are honor students or bear some distinction, who would alternate watches through their day and night. They would give their hometowns the uplifting task of sending them. Jackie would supply the snacks at Arlington. The memorial comes to life! A better idea, suggests Doug, is to send our bar mitzvah class there for a whole year. Good for them and even better for their parents.

We are starting to practice sermons. Mark tells us excitedly that no blacks, women, Jews, or Connecticut people have ever been our president. He has a solution. A kid should be president. It will be better, he insists. Maybe he's right, maybe no one should serve in any political office throughout the world if they're past thirteen. Perhaps ten, I think, to save that waste of time about sex scandals.

We begin work on one of the great Sabbath prayers that precedes the opening of the Ark where the Torah is kept. "You kids have to learn this," says Doug, "because—and it's sad—someday you won't be living here anymore, and you'll join a synagogue some other place on earth and, as an honor, you'll be asked to say this prayer by an old Jew in the congregation." "That'll be you, Doug!" says Adam. We're to know the prayer before the end of the month. "That's Halloween," says Mark. "We'll be out doing mischief." "Remember," says Doug, "in the old days we didn't go out much on Mischief Night. Do you think that a hundred years ago, in Russia, Jewish kids ran out and draped toilet paper around the Cossacks' stables?"

Then Doug gives advice about sermons. He tells a story about a young rabbi who was proud of his recent sermon. "It was excellent!" he said. "Compared to what?" asked an older rabbi. "Why, to other sermons." "And compared," asked the elder, "to saying nothing?"

Two girls in the class younger than us give a passionate and well-organized sermon, recounting their distress that soccer games are insensitively scheduled on Jewish holidays. Coaches get mad if the kids don't show up. I imagine that if these girls warned the coaches that they would miss key games, they wouldn't get good positions on the team. An awkward situation. Doug suggests that we write letters of protest to the local coaches. Funny, he says, things work out better when the coaches are Jewish. Maybe we need a few more. Infiltration.

On Sunday, Adam doesn't have his notebook. "I don't have it and I don't know where it is," he offers in a challenging manner. The question today is, again, why are you to be a bar mitzvah? All the others except Aaron and Adam have the same answer: "My parents want it." Aaron says his parents yell at him, so he wants "to be a man." Adam won't budge from "I don't know." We study the new loose-leaf sheets for our notebooks that list reasons. Number 10 is my choice: "It's showing my connection with my people and my ancestors." Adam grudgingly picks Number 7: "I like the presents and the party." Aaron chooses the first half of Number 2: "It's okay. I'm not sure I want to do it, but my parents want me to . . . ." The second half, which he does not mention, is "and I want to make them happy." Small rebellion.

A home video camera appears, and we are to repeat these questions and answers as interviews. Adam says that's nonsense, but steps forward when a cameraman is needed.

At assembly, Doug does his three-minute improvised sermon, based on a small checkered triangle of cloth that is brought in. The subject is how we are all connected. Another clue is a small toad, and Doug remarks that in life there are obstacles that we must hop over, then asks the boy who brought the toad to go outside and release it. The sermon will carry into the fields.

We drive to the synagogue to rehearse for the Friday night

service, which our class will conduct. I take Mark and Adam and Sara in my pickup, which has two jump seats in the back. When they climb in, the scene shifts abruptly, in my imagination, to that scene in the film *Mr. Hulot's Holiday* when the unfortunate Hulot lights a match to explore the interior of a shed and finds out suddenly that it's packed with the Bastille Day explosives and fireworks. When we arrive, Doug also seems dazed as his four students race out of his van. At the rehearsal he is patient, but his patience is stretched. Adam keeps saying no, Jami doesn't want to do this and that, but eventually Doug gets all of them on the bema and starts a reasonable rehearsal. Mark won't sing because he claims that they make fun of him. Curious, because he had been thrown out of class the week before for singing the prayers operatically, hands clasped like a diva. It wasn't simple insubordination when he didn't stop: once he got started he couldn't stop. Now he's devised a way to come out of his shoes when he walks, and that masterstroke cripples most efforts at serious work. Adam finds a way to make Mark laugh by just chiming in on the final syllable of each word. Bit by bit we get through it. I'm just the transportation, because I can't be at that particular service. I watch and commiserate with Doug. Doug calls out, "*Hey, easy,* that's my bema!" but is never harsher than that. Ultimately, and Doug knows that this will happen, the kids don't want to let each other down, and when he says that anyone who wants to leave can do so, they don't leave. They can't anyway, they don't have cars. On the way back to the annex there are birds darting and swooping, the entire flock shifting color instantly from black to white as they wheel. My passengers hang out the windows yelling "Let me in!" to the whole town. Then they all laugh and apologize to me for "being impossible twelve-year-olds."

At the annex, Doug tells me that his mother wanted him to be a doctor or lawyer. She urged this even after she was convinced that his rabbinical aspirations were serious. She told him to just get the degree in law or medicine, he didn't have to practice. My own mother thought she could set my feet on a more respectable path than theater by putting me through architectural school. Long after I was successful in stage and theatrical design and earning well, she kept at me. "I'll pay for the school," she said, about once every six months. When I was fifty I had a good idea. "Mom," I said, "architects drink." She never mentioned the matter again.

My son, Dan, is better at that kind of manipulation than I am. He wanted a dog, but Leonora and I, then city dwellers, resisted. One day he told us that a friend had offered him a free puppy from a litter that was half Doberman, half wolf. "Good grief, Dan! If we get a dog it will have to be small!" "Okay, Dad, as long as it has a heart that beats."

The next Wednesday I learn that the Friday evening service went beautifully. Success hasn't made a notable change in my classmates. Jami works with concentration during the session, prying up a playing-card-size piece of Formica from the surface of our worktable. Adam snaps his loose-leaf notebook's rings and zips himself into his leather jacket again, giving us his straw-stuffed headless scarecrow impression.

We discuss the values of the Jewish people as a large family: love of the whole family, love of learning, common roots, 3700 years of history, survival of suffering. "Fund-raising," Jami adds.

At our service I sit next to Ben, a boy in the class below ours who tends to both liven up and slow down our proceedings. There is, in fact, an opening ritual to these group classes. They do not begin with a prayer, as I said above. They start: "Ben, sit down. Ben, sit down. Ben!" I learn that the root of the word *yeshiva*, (school), is *shiv*, to sit down. When we read Hebrew, Ben seems fluent, and I'm envious. Today, Doug has a banjo and says that he is taking lessons. Many times during the service he takes it up and then puts it down again, at no time striking a note.

Norman Hanenbaum appears. He's been a music teacher in this area, and I've met many of his grateful former students. He's in our klezmer band and has started a synagogue choir, which we name "The Norman Tabernacle Choir." He sets up a keyboard, and we rehearse "The Latke Song," which we might sing, I suppose if we're good enough, at Chanukah. That's when these delicious potato pancakes appear.

> *I am so mixed up that I cannot tell you,*
> *I'm sitting in this blender turning brown,*
> *I've made friends with the onions and the flour,*
> *And the cook is scouting o-il in town.*

> CHORUS: *I am a latke, I'm a latke,*
> *And I am waiting for Chanukah to come,*
> *I am a latke, I'm a latke, etc.*

Debbie Friedman wrote this, and she sings it exuberantly on a CD. Try it with a rhumba beat.

On the 6th of November there's the usual excitement before class. Ben: "That boy has a knife! He's practicing to be a *moyle*." I peer past Adam's feet up on the table as we make slow progress, mostly with the *V'ahavta* prayer. I read shakily but acceptably, and Doug asks for appreciation from the class, considering my late start. I have a dry mouth from nervousness and appreciate the

Gummi Bears that Doug spins across the table to reward my reading and to remind us that the study of Torah is sweet. Then bad news: we'll have a Boston overnight in February.

As we leave our classroom, I overhear Ben saying, "I got kicked out of class again." Doug draws me aside and tells me that I might prefer to miss the overnight. He is kind to point this out. The overnight will include, he guesses rightly, running up and down the hallways screaming, strip poker, etc. Then he coaches me on prayers. "You know," he says, "Hebrew's a *hard* language!"

Chapter 10

* * *

EMPTY SEATS

T APED TO A WALL in the annex are eleven crayon pictures of Doug, drawn by the seven-year-olds. They are drawn on the coarse, tinted paper doled out for crayon work, and the subjects are Doug leading services; Doug lighting the Menorah; Doug eating challah; Doug sitting; Doug reading the Torah; Doug playing with Mical, his older daughter, which picture includes a doll that Doug holds like a ventriloquist's dummy, or maybe that's Mical and the other figure is a self-portrait of the young artist. All show Doug smiling. These drawings are diligently and boldly made, with Doug's full body filling the frame in almost all, and they accurately portray clothing, eyeglasses, *kippah,* etc. They show admiration for him. The five I haven't mentioned are of one subject: Doug hard at work at one of his hobbies, magic, which he shares with us on occasions that involve children. He is doing the Floating Dreidel Trick. A dreidel is a small wooden top spun by kids at Chanukah. In each of these crayon portraits the second finger of his left hand is featured, and that consistently keen observation is remarkable. A heavy black line loops that finger and then descends and is tied to the suspended top. Kids can't be expected to differentiate line widths between a thread and a string in a medium as coarse as wax crayon, but any subtlety here lies between a rope and a hawser. "Rabbi Doug," I say, "there seems to be a sort of coherence here, I mean as to how the dreidel levitates." "I paid over a hundred dollars for that darn trick," Doug mutters.

Some things don't change. I see Doug as a tugboat trying to maneuver Ben into dock. The service starts as an *azan,* which is the call of the muezzin to the flock from a minaret: "Ben, Ben, sit down." This can be repeated four times, in the four compass directions. Ben is complimentary to Doug, and Doug thanks him. "Right, Ben, but we can admire each other after services."

Today it is my turn to practice giving a sermon. It is Wednesday, and the two oldest classes will be there. I arrive at the annex early, but some kids are already racing around the assembly room and leaping on the donated stuffed furniture. From the front window we look over the parking lot, shared with the dry cleaners, and cars arrive to drop off kids or clothes and then are driven away. The kids from Durham erupt from one van. That town is far enough away to require carpooling. The students inside call out the names of the boys and girls now racing around the parking lot. The usual teasing: the van's springs jump up when Ben gets off, they say, and of course it's not that Ben is so heavy, but his personality is formidable. "The earth trembles!" says one boy as Ben steers himself toward the door downstairs. The scene becomes indelible to me when I hear Doug saying aloud, almost in a chant, "How lovely it is to see these children come in happiness to study Torah," and suddenly there is a glow that surrounds Doug, and it could be

a century ago, and he could have a long beard, and our sunny annex could be one of those lithographs of rooms with a scholar-
teacher, and he has a sad El Greco face, and a blond boy in the front
row looks raptly in a different direction, or admiringly at his
teacher, and other boys read from books and scrolls. I think of the
Japanese word *ongaeshi,* meaning the act or necessity, even compulsion, for a master to teach, to pass on knowledge. I hope that
today's class runs smoothly. Doug's mood might change, and he
could quote his granny again: "*Vildehayes!*"

In my sermon I tell Doug's story about Rabbi Akiva, who lived
45–135 C.E. Doug intended this story to be encouraging to me.
Akiva, a shepherd, took refuge from the midday sun in a cave,
probably to eat his lunch. He noticed a drip from the ceiling that
had worn a depression in the stone floor. If drops of water can do
that, he reasoned, I can learn. So he went to school with his son
and learned the alphabet. It took him ten years, and then he went
on to become one of our greatest sages. The kids understand that I
might need ten years to learn the Hebrew aleph-bet, and I get my
laugh. Then I tell my favorite story, a story, I say, that explains all
stories, and perhaps they know it because it is so often told.

Once upon a time there was a miracle-working rabbi who
could go to a certain clearing in the woods, face in a certain direction, and say magic words. He would get a miracle. Then generations passed, and the magic words were forgotten. When a miracle
was needed, the rabbi of that time went to the woods and found
the clearing. He faced in the proper direction and said to God that
he knew he was in the right place and facing in the right direction,
but the magic words were lost to him, and yet, please, grant him
the miracle. The miracle was granted. Generations passed, and
when a miracle was needed the rabbi of that time went to the

woods and found the clearing and said to God that he knew that he was in the right place, and he knew that the rabbis of old had magic words and faced a certain way, but he could do no more than stand before God in the clearing and ask a miracle. The miracle was granted. Finally the woods were cut down, and after many years the new rabbi could only go into the village square and tell God that he knew that there had been woods and a clearing, but they were gone, and knowledge had come down through generations that there had been a direction to face and magic words to say, all now lost. But he needed a miracle. And God granted him the miracle.

God put men and women on earth, it is said, because he loves stories.

Questions follow these sermons. Ben asks if Rabbi Doug will play the tambourine at my party? "Yes." Then a young student with a layered haircut asks me when will it be, and that's easy. Mark asks how do I *really* feel about being with all these youngsters, and I say I like it, but I wish there wasn't so darn much interruption of the lessons, and every kid in the room smiles.

On this Wednesday we are a group of eighteen, plus a few teachers and Doug. There are about twenty-five extra folding chairs set up in the room. I have a problem with empty seats and am distracted from my sermon. I once conducted a memorial service for my beloved theater partner Mack Scism. We did it in Palmer Auditorium at Connecticut College, and we set up chairs like these in a semicircle on the stage itself. Perhaps thirty people came to listen and to contribute. We spoke from a lectern downstage, facing upstage. At one point, when Ted Chapin was speaking, I walked to the back of the seats and listened from there. The large and empty auditorium was behind Ted, and this is a common picture to all stage workers, who listen or watch the director or choreographer or conductor with the empty house as background. So much of our time is spent this way that we do not feel, as audiences do, that the curtain rises on a show. To us that front curtain, unseen during the weeks of rehearsal, comes down. It is shy, appearing briefly but ominously, and when it first descends most of us have never seen it, front or back. When first rehearsals are over and we're ready to perform, it comes down ("in," we say) at the "Half hour!" warning before the show starts. "Curtain's in," someone announces, and we know that we may safely walk or warm up behind it while the audience enters. To them, it will go up to reveal our show. To us, it has come in briefly to conceal us. It arrives again for intermission, and after the show it is in after curtain calls for perhaps ten minutes as the audience leaves. Then it is raised and disappears into the flys until the half-hour warning before the next performance.

I looked at all the empty seats as Ted spoke, and they began to fill for me with the people Mack knew. Slowly materializing were the Native Americans that watched as Mack, an infant in the hands of his missionary mother, was used to demonstrate soapy enemas. Mostly squaws, so Mack told me. Then Mack's loyal employees began to fill the seats, and then those friends I met during his years directing a theater in Oklahoma. I knew many of his subscribers: they entered and took their seats. There were the architects and workers with whom I helped him build his theater. Mack's board betrayed him, and he left Oklahoma and came to work with us, and soon filling the seats were the groups that gathered for his colorful explanations of our style. Next to file in were our staff and his friends here in the Northeast, those not at our service that day. The theater seats were filled with the phantoms of the people he had helped and to whom he had been kind.

Mack charmed all who knew him, and I'm inclined to say that word in the older, mystic sense. Leonora's love for him was always at the flood, and they shared the gift of warming lives, particularly of single people who were in some ways cut off, as she had been in her childhood and as he had become after his life's work had been cut down. Leonora said, "Mack could charm the pants off the wall-paper."

Mack had no use for religion. He struggled to fill a theater in a city where almost half the population were forbidden to enjoy it. When we were looking for a new home, and found some churches for sale, a member of my board asked how such buildings were de-sanctified. "Hell," said Mack, "I just walks in." In his Oklahoma speech, the five words needed ten syllables.

Concerns with empty seats are not uncommon for someone who has spent his life trying to fill them. Were those Mack's angels filling that auditorium? They showed up. Did anyone else see them? If I could see his, are mine visible, surrounding me?

I won't worry about empty seats at my bar mitzvah. When Leonora sends out invitations, the return rate is always about 115 percent.

Back in class, the lesson of the day is about God's concern with good and evil. "What if you don't believe in God?" asks Jami. Doug answers yes, this lesson presupposes that, but listen anyway. Then, why did the writer change the prayer from the sense that God created good and evil, in Isaiah, to "God created all things," which is in the prayer book in this passage based on Isaiah?

"What is evil?" asks Doug. "Boys!" says Sara. "Adolescents?"

asks Doug. "Hitler!" shouts Jami. One answer to the question of this subtle change relates to Zoroastrians, who had two Gods, one for good and one for evil. To meet this two-God challenge, which arose after Isaiah, our belief and the text asserts that our one God does all, but we don't want to be specific and say that He created evil.

Doug has to leave the room for a moment, and the kids cut up. "You won't squeal on us, will you, Dave?" asks Mark. "Hell no," I say, "I'm your classmate."

During the next Wednesday's news session we learn that the pet chinchilla has finally arrived, and that a boy ran into one of our teachers at DisneyWorld. Today Ben gives the sermon. He's nervous and says so. His short sermon is about Jewish humor. We're funny, he says. Many comics come from us: Seinfeld, Adam Sandler. He is succinct and draws no conclusions. He just ends up saying that we're funny. Well, I wonder, Why are we funny? Do we have a choice? And shouldn't we be grateful that God gave us this second greatest of gifts, humor? Ben did not mention the comics that come to my mind, the old-timers like Sid Caesar, Danny Kaye, Henny Youngman, Jack Benny. But who remembers anything anymore? That complaint has surely dogged our species since the second generation of cavepersons. I feel more and more like Uncle Eddie. "Nothing's worth remembering." Wrong. It's worth it, Eddie, but who does?

I like the pageantry we have in our ceremonies. We learn about the different offices, the name for the person who holds the Torah, the *hagbah,* then the *gelilah,* who, after the reading, puts back the band that keeps the scroll from unrolling and restores its cover and ornaments. I love to see the Torah come out of the Ark cradled in our arms and then paraded about and cared for. I know many who claim that their fascination with theater originated with the Catholic Church's pageantry—not just in the Mass but in the glow of the colored windows, in the soaring architecture, and in the presence of statues of suffering and entranced people. When I was a student in London I enjoyed the colorful displays of the Royal Family. This was not long after the Second World War, and the family and the tradition they represented had been an inspiration to most of the nation. I stood in the rain all night with Norman Geschwind, next to the Carriageway, and in the morning, on my twenty-third birthday, the Queen rode to her coronation. What a parade! First, at dawn, in drizzle, a runner came by carrying a sign that said Everest had been climbed—or was it that the four-minute mile had been run, or both? Then the sun came out. Exotic people from around the world marched by in dazzling costumes, then the Queen, so beautiful and so happy that day, with luminous skin that could have been made of porcelain, and she waved right at us.

Gone, most of it, but I have a solution to loss. I can sail out of sight of land, where the world is as it was when the oceans were made, and I can use an instrument that is a close cousin of Columbus' astrolabe to tell me my latitude from the heights of the sun at noon or the North Star at dusk or dawn. But how many can afford this? Discouraging? No, the sermons of my classmates are as idealistic as were our talks and essays fifty-four years ago. (The magnetic variation of the Earth, measured on Long Island Sound where I sailed as a boy, has changed a full degree in that span of my life.) Today the young people speak of their eagerness for an informed and active life, just as we did, and they speak of injustices that must be corrected, and these are injustices that many of us never noticed those many years ago, when the colorfully dressed black men marched for the Queen more than forty-five years ago.

They were the incarnation of photographs in *The National Geographic,* where you could show topless photographs if the women were brown skinned.

Gone, most of it, Uncle Eddie. Now that son of the Queen's, the one with big ears, wants to be his mistress' nappy, figure it out, and I see him with a string sticking out of the top of his head. To quote Chekhov, in a good translation, "Strictly speaking, to hell with it."

Chapter 11

*   *   *

MY MOTHER'S LAST
INSTRUCTIONS

I RARELY VISITED MY mother without telephoning first, a consideration that even the closest relative deserves. She was living alone in her big house in Norwalk. Her hearing was poor, and I didn't want to startle her. She usually sat in the kitchen, where there was a loud doorbell. One day I did come by unexpectedly. She didn't respond, and after some time it occurred to me to look through the glass panels that flanked the front door. I could see into the living room, where Mom was stretched out on the sofa. Dead! It didn't occur to me at first that she was napping. I assumed the worst because I had never seen her lying down, not once, since I was a tiny child, when I would sometimes crawl into her bed in the early morning.

Before the Massacre in the Stamford diner, my son and I were planning a sea voyage, a six-month sabbatical needed by me and a well-timed full year for my son, who had finished college and was indecisive. Mom kept shifting the dates of her move from Norwalk to her "residence." When I said I would leave on October 4th, she said she'd move on October 5th. When I changed to the 6th, she insisted on the 7th, so I left and she moved. The moving men set down her furniture in the apartment in Stamford, and it never budged until six years later when we moved her to her final home, a new "full-care facility" in North Branford. We chose this because, among other reasons, it permitted Mom to keep a few of her antiques in her room. She particularly wanted a large photograph of her mother. My maternal grandmother, widowed early and left with eleven children, took over the family haberdashery in Bridgeport and sent every child to college. When Mom herself was first a widow, she talked of my father, her Mortimer, and then became more involved with her grandchildren and finally her great-grandchildren, and I never again heard Dad's name. Then perhaps a station of her journey was marked by the day her final few teeth were removed. My brother supervised that conscientiously, but he was in a fury when he brought her home. The dentist had failed to inform him before the extractions that she had a rare condition, a malformed palate, and could not be fitted for false teeth. Mom's vanity never recovered from the toothlessness and that was the day, I believe, when she saw the road before her straighten out. Then the companion on this road became her mother, and until she died, Mom's thoughts and much of her conversation was of her.

Stamford, and then finally Branford, were on my way to New York City, where I had much to do, and often I drove to visit Mom and then parked at the station and completed the trip by train. Sometimes I only napped during our visits, and she told me that seeing me sleeping again gave her intense pleasure. I know this

pleasure now. I tend to wake at three in the morning and sometimes have trouble recapturing sleep. But not if my son or daughter is in the next room, or if a grandson is asleep in the other berth
in our small boat. I see how restless, even purposeless, my life has
seemed since my children left home.

Mom could make water boil faster by staring at it, but her eagle
glance soothed me when I napped, as she sat and looked steadily at
me until I woke. Often we held hands as I read to her. Poetry was
her favorite. Something had gone wrong in her eyes and she could
no longer read. But her alert posture told us that neither reading
nor television, nor much else from outside her own head, was
needed. Her memory of poetry was extraordinary, and her favorite
was a section from Longfellow's *Morituri Salutamus,* written near
the end of his life. (Speak of overlap, of the generational relay:
Longfellow died only twenty-six years before Mom was born.) My
mother had memorized this before the First World War. The problem was that she couldn't alter her pace or start or stop in the middle. Once she raised anchor, the poem went under full sail to the
end, and any grounding required a totally fresh start to the voyage.
I guessed that Mom would like this poem read at her funeral, so I
transcribed it at my top writing speed and with many repetitions
by Mom, which she enjoyed but which always restarted from the
top, no matter how far along we were in the poem when she out-
stripped me. She dried up at the sight of a recording device, so I
had to write out the poem in longhand because I couldn't find it in
any anthology. It was buried in the longer poem. When I finally
found it and checked it, Mom's version was perfect, not one hair
out of place after three-quarters of a century.

In her ending days, Mom never lost her quick mind nor her
timing. We finally sat in her last room in North Branford, stuffed

with her furniture, her wheelchair skimming by the Chippendale with not an inch to spare. The large and ornately framed sepia photo of her mother hung where she could see it when she woke in the morning. A nurse came in and announced that part of the entry procedure was a memory test, which she would now provide. Mom knew perfectly well that her short-term memory was shot, but she was a fighter, and she paused only a second to gather her forces.

"Ah," she opened, "*memory*. What does that word mean? I've forgotten!"

She fooled no one, nor intended to, but the nurse was staggered, and Mom observed this with triumph. The lady in the white smock had underestimated my mother, and the opening broadside had carried away her rigging.

"Well," said the nurse, "let's start. What day is this?"

"That, young lady, is not memory, that is current events!"

"True, Mrs. Hays, true. Well, perhaps . . . perhaps you can tell me when you were born—no—I know you don't remember that yourself. I mean the, no, not the actual event, but perhaps you can remember the day and the year; you know, your birthday—what they told you."

"Of course, young lady. January twenty-third." Then, with only the slightest pause, "David, test *your* memory! Do you remember the year?"

"Sure, Mom, 1898."

"That's right! Good for you."

The nurse checked "correct" on her form.

"Well, finally, Mrs. Hays, do you remember your last phone number?"

"Why should I? I lived alone, I never called myself! Anyway,

Nurse, the only important numbers are those of my boys. Do you
know those?"

"Of course."

The perfect pause, then: "And what are they?" Again the perfect
pause, slightly longer: "AHA!"

Mom was the second patient in the new facility, and she set the
same standard for the staff that she set for all of us and Uncle Eddie. You measured up or the devil with you. She lasted six months.
Twice she had to go to the hospital in New Haven, and the second
time it took them three hours to release her. Old woman, dressed
and ready, sitting for three hours in a wheelchair by the nurses' station, plucking at her lip. (That's a habit I have too, and my daughter cries out with irritation when she sees in me my mother's old
age.) Two doctors had the authority to release her, but we were told
that one doctor was off that day and the other was in an all-day
meeting. Finally, seething with rage, I had an inspiration, and said,
"It's a fund-raising meeting, isn't it?" Mom cackled at the obvious
bulls-eye and at the turmoil caused by what a hospital doesn't
want known when care is at a standstill. There's nothing wrong
with fund-raising, but it's not part of the Hippocratic oath and
fails to enhance a hospital's image at certain moments. The physi-
cian quickly appeared and signed her out.

Mom didn't forget that, and when she was sick again she refused to go back, choosing instead to die.

I had stopped by in the morning and tried to feed her, encouraged by concerned nurses. She seemed well, and I didn't perceive
her stubbornness as ominously as the experienced women. "You're
too tall" said Mom, and she laughed to the five-foot-eleven nurse
who sat beside me, and then looked at her with that "you're beautiful" smile of hers. I didn't hear her laugh again. We were reached

at a fancy function in New York that evening. I phoned Julia, who was living in the city, and she and I drove up. Leonora would follow in the morning. And so I arrived in my tuxedo for this more formal occasion. My brother and Sue were there, with one of their sons and his wife.

"Talk to her, David, maybe she'll respond to you," said Sue, who had been a fine nurse and keeps current in her reading. I said "Mom, wake up, you have visitors," or some such, but the comatose woman didn't respond.

"Try again," said Sue, but I didn't. Let her go, her own way. Mom had crossed a threshold, why go back at ninety-four and then have to cross again, perhaps with pain? I thought of Peer Gynt, who sped his mother to the castle in the sky above the northern lights, riding her bed like a sleigh.

Like so many old people, Mom had waited for a special day, a holiday, and had then let go. The old, like the very young, know that refusing to eat is one of the few ways to dominate their keepers. She had stopped eating the day after her birthday.

My brother and his family members stood to leave. It was past midnight. "They go at two in the morning," said Sue.

Julia and I talked small talk and held Mom's hands. Her breathing was steady and light. She wasn't restless in the bed. The photographic image of her mother looked on the daughter with the sad sepia eyes of a lovely young woman, the photograph taken 112 years before. I'm sure that Mom remembered her as that young and handsome. I was taken to meet her when I was four, shortly before she died. I remember how she resembled the image of another old woman whom I can see clearly and recognize from many photographs, Queen Victoria. I remember that there was a light behind her, probably a floor lamp, and that there was a glow on a lacy cap that she wore, and that her face was in shadow as she bent down to look at me. I remember her pungent smell, sharp and dark, an old woman's smell. I remember the rasp of her full, stiff black dress. I remember romping on a sloping green lawn with other children. Perhaps with my cousin Janet, my age, the "I'll-show-you-mine-if-you-show-me-yours" cousin, who put her finger against her lips and led me to a room in the old house and pushed open a door, stifling giggles. Uncle Eddie, a young man, lay fast asleep on his stomach, naked, taking his afternoon nap. I saw hairy buttocks horizontal, at eye level.

Leonora says, "You were a peeping Dick!"

Recently Leonora and I were driving through one of the nicer sections of Bridgeport where we were to attend the presentation of an honorary doctorate. A friend had given $300,000 to a local university—she could at least be called Doctor.

"There—look! That's the house!" I cried.

"How can you be sure? It must be—what?—fifty years ago?"

"Yes—no—fifty-eight. I was there only once, for a weekend. But that is *it*."

When I asked Mom, she remembered the old family address, and I was right. The memory test hadn't asked for information from before the turn of the century. Now, stroking her hair, not as white as mine, I too am thinking of her mother, and of mysteries I'll never understand. Disconnected thoughts in sadness and exhaustion. The mystery that troubles me most of all about my mother, and it may someday tell me more about myself than about her, is why she never played the piano. She could play and sight-read, and she sang in a clear and sweet voice. I heard her only once. She loved Gilbert and Sullivan. Perhaps she felt that the world was too sad. She hungered for the different arts and needed them, but perhaps she felt it was not her amateur place to practice them.

At two in the morning, I told Julia that I needed a Tums from my car and walked out into the cold and still January air. The door latched shut against me. I hadn't expected that; I had never been there at night. Mom's window was on the ground floor, and I tapped on it. Julia opened the curtain and then met me at the door.

"Grandma died. There was a shift in her rhythm, and then a wince, like a quick little pain, and then she stopped breathing."

Again I stroked my mother's hair, full and soft, and I said, "Mom, you're still so beautiful." Julia was holding her hand. "Sorry," I said to Julia, "I must have frightened you so." "Your tap on the window came about three seconds after she died. I almost crashed through the ceiling." We walked to the nurses' station. "Dad, it was so like your mother; she waited until the one moment you were out of the room. She didn't want to disturb you."

A year later we buried Eddie's urn at the unveiling of Mom's headstone, which only needed the final date of her life. Her name had been carved next to my father's, committed to granite for thirty years, and now that commitment was met with a few final numbers. Richard had approved my plan to bury Eddie's urn in the one remaining plot, which adjoined Mom's. There was no other single person left in our family that would use the old Brooklyn cemetery. Eddie's ashes, undisturbed in their box, had been under my desk for four years, his whole body turned to the talcum of his resented footprints. His life had appeared to be so uneventful that I couldn't think of any cherished place to scatter them. Down the shower at last? An awful thought. Around that diner in Stamford? I hadn't even liked Eddie until I became his conservator, his father, so to speak. Then I loved him. Figure it out. Mom hadn't reacted much at his death, nor at the deaths of anyone in her own family. She ignored death, including her own, unless the death was of any young person, perhaps the classmate of a grandchild, a person she hardly knew.

The chief of the cemetery troweled out the grave for Eddie, eight inches square and about eighteen inches deep in the soft earth. We are beyond the glacial invasion in this southern part of Long Island, and there were no boulders to shift. The urn was lowered and covered. Farewell, Eddie of the poached balls, tempus fidgeted, Tom Sawyer.

We placed pebbles on my parents' headstone, and there was a moment to think. No speeches here, the rabbi will speak briefly, and I'd asked for Hebrew, the old words, though Mom and Dad and Eddie had not known the prayers that I am now learning. I remembered that when I was about six I told Mom that I didn't want to die and be buried. Her answers were always true to the mark; she grasped the child's operative thought and soothed me. "You don't have to be buried. There are places where you can lie with beautiful flowers." Later in my young life she would come home from the theater or any collection of art that thrilled her and describe what she had seen. Her last sentence was always the same: "Nothing you can't do, David." But there were tart pronouncements as well, for between the riches there were stiffer layers that held her together like a lasagna, layers that were al dente. Out of them came simple statements, not gems: "The devil with it," or an arsenal of quips all starting with "Humph!" or my favorite, "That's UN-necessary," applied to all things scatological, for example when Daniel, age four, said "shit" in front of her. "What did that child say?" she cried. "S-H-I-T, Grandma," whispered seven-year-old Julia into her ear. "That," said Mom, "was UN-necessary." Or one constant that I first remember from when I was about four, just thirty years earlier in time than Daniel's four-letter-word day. "I wish I'd never been born," she said. When I was that young, this hurt me, because to my simple thinking I was hearing that my life wasn't reward enough for hers.

I looked at the new carving on the headstone and the small heap of earth over the penetration that we have made for Eddie. I recalled a statement that was frequent but unusually ordinary, even coarse, for this woman who never returned to New York City after she saw shorts worn on Fifth Avenue. She would say, "Over my dead body." Now, with a start, I saw what I'd created. When all was said and done, which meant at that moment, Mom didn't like dull Eddie. His ashes lie about thirty inches above her coffin and fifteen inches to her left. I'm sorry, Mom, and I know you forgive me, but I hear you, perhaps shrieking in the tones of that dreadful parrot in *Treasure Island*, "Over my dead body!"

* * *

MY YOUNG LADY

A T TUTORIAL, Doug tells me a story from medieval times of a community in which there was one terrible anti-Semite, a horrible and damaging man, and the elders decided that their only recourse was to kidnap him, and they did so. He was blindfolded and taken to a basement and put in a chair, and obvious stove noises and smells began. He asked in terror what was going to happen to him, and he was told that lead was being heated and, when molten, would be poured down his throat for all that he had said. Finally they said, "It's ready," and they pulled back the head of the terrified pleading man and forced open his mouth. They began pouring in the liquid, and the man instantly realized it was honey. "And it must be this way in my class," says Doug, "because the teaching of Torah must always be sweet."

An older rabbi's advice: if only at this age we could lock them up and free them in a year; how sweet they become. "And remember," says Doug, "that at their age of rebellion, the parents send them here, and what better revolt against the parents than to piss on religion because that is something that comes down from them. Besides, religion is a great target because it won't ground them, stop them from going to the mall."

In class, Adam is vigorously trying to color the white raised letters on his sneaker's sole with a brown Magic Marker.

Last week's happenings: a girl went to a hotel that had real trees growing in the lobby. Mark also went to a hotel, and in the lobby there were two men talking; a big familiar guy, one of the tallest in the National Basketball Association, and a smaller man. Mark asked the big man if he could pose with him for a snapshot, then asked the small man (politely, I'm sure) if he would move aside, and that happened. Later Mark realized that the small man was Billy Crystal. Then Doug must again defend his hairline. He offers a prize for a project due next week. Ben: "Your hairpiece!" Imagine a spiritual leader with a hairpiece! Question: do you need a yarmulke if you are wearing a toupee?

At a Judaica store in West Hartford I get the expected answers to my questions. No, we don't have "inspirational tapes" like the Christians, we have study tapes, examining the Talmud and so forth. We do not have a proselytizing religion. Yes, there are a few tapes, mostly Orthodox, urging us to be more devout, meaning that we must study more. Some of the rabbis who make these tapes speak in that oily tone of ministers that I don't like, she says. But I enjoy the parallel: devout equals study.

I go to the annex three times a week, twice with my classmates and once for tutorial with Doug. I go with joy. My concern for my classmates has become an alliance that has swept me away. My investment would be ordinary and everyday for them in their rapid lives full of associations and disassociations, of yearly and even seasonal new friends. Their populations shift monthly in their sports teams, their music lessons, in the changing faces as they race from room to room in their schools to regroup. I don't go home now to the shouting growth and skirmishes of my then younger family, when that ship was on its voyage with each shifting wave to be met and often leaky enough to demand full time at the pumps. Now I am in a harbor where the winds and skies may change, but my anchor is down and my few real friends are on board. I see my young classmates, the Hormone Hurricanes, twice a week. And now at this moment of spring for them, this rich turmoil in their own minds and bodies, I too am stirred, my anchor drags, and old debris rises to the surface.

I am accepted but have little role in this dog pack, a mobile hierarchy as they jockey for position by challenging Doug or each other. The challenges to Doug are sharp, but the acts of insubordination that he gently tolerates are already waning. Debbie, our Sunday teacher, lacks the rank of rabbi, and a triumph over her is not as large a prize. In her classes the elbowing is within the pack, just high spirits and rarely directed toward her authority. She has a shaky but intact string of victories. I try to help her keep in control, but in quiet ways that won't make me a teacher's pet. I tail along, back of the pack.

No elixir salesman could lure me back to the pain of youth that now surrounds me if I had to carry back my carpetbag of experience. These are not deprived youngsters, indeed, they are privileged, but some have had disappointments. They have had or seen the agonies of split families, a cloud over young people now. The child of one such family asked Doug if they could say Kaddish, the great prayer for the dead, over their living but absent father. "Isn't that chilling?" said Doug to me. Yet, a heavenly armor protects them, yes, these kids have built-in defenses, their own elixir, perhaps named Grow-No-Matter-What. Thick armor is needed at their ages: they bear what they rightly perceive as insulting criticism, sarcasm sometimes, from their teachers; they lose fights, verbal and physical, in the school yards; they are jeered or yah-yahed! by schoolmates; they suffer overheard whispers that they are ugly, creepy, a nig or a yid; if they make a new and poorly ranked friend, they will be eliminated from the clique of the most popular girl or boy; they lose on the field by missing a goal or letting one slip by under the lifted-to-heaven-eyes of their exasperated and unsympathetic teammates, full of venomous blame, who humiliated them anyway by choosing them last. At the end of each day they are supposed to be serene at supper, and asked how the day went, they say "Fine," and leave it at that, the question doesn't enter their private world, they think no more about it. Then they are instructed to do homework, then there's piano practice; half of them go to bed terrified that their bosom will never grow (or that it will pop out in a wrong style); the other half worries that, when the first half does indeed grow bosoms, they'll be left behind and insecure with their later changes, and they sense that they will be alone for the passage, understanding even at that age that manliness is supposed to be lonelier than the sisterhood shared by girls. These youngsters wake up to yells for being late for breakfast or school; they set out for classes sometimes only half prepared for a quiz, and they bravely face this. Ten times a day they pass through social or academic barbed-wire gates that would tear off gobs of my flesh. Faced with only one such gate, I would find it a trauma. Ten times a day I would march upset out of my office, lie down to rest with a Valium, have a drink if I were a drinker, have a sundae if I had fat attacks—I do—and feel fervently sorry for myself. After just one of the many daily trips through these wringers I would lose a hat or a pencil, and I would stand and roar out my rage and—I have done this—weep from frustration at a little thing that focuses the moment, if not the blame. Some days these kids get out into the hallway after fifty minutes of humiliation that would today put me in the emergency ward, and they shrug free and are off to the next activity. I know that I have none of their defenses. I've molted the adolescent's skin, so thick to these routine insults, yet so thin to others. Bonding with my classmates to the small extent that I can, I feel distant vibrations of pain that are almost unbearable.

My classmates. I look around in assembly at the other classes, and they too are beautiful to me, but to their blunt-speaking contemporaries and to themselves they are fat, ugly, stupid. In the slim list I've tried to reconstruct of their daily agonies, there is no knowing what will scar them. Myself, I have few areas left to be scarred. Knock wood, I've come through, if I die before my children or grandchildren. I do not have to bear now what my classmates routinely hear; comments such as "She's so ugly no one will marry her" come not only from kids, they are overheard from parents. I knew parents once who said to me, right in front of their girl, that she was no world-beater. But when she was sixteen they gave her a Porsche, and certain parts of her life picked up. I do not have the overwhelming loneliness, the coiled-up misery of the lost or rejected child, and now I feel it keenly for the first time in my life, I feel it for my classmates. I did not feel this for my children because Julia was not troubled, Dan covered up well, and life roared along too fast. I was steering on a fast road and barely looked around at the passengers, and this failure to catch time and slow it is the most haunting failure in my memory. Now, in my new Merlin life, adrift in the sea of my youthful classmates, I sit in assembly and hurt for time badly spent; I could cry. Well, what the hell, we made it, they will, inoculated by youth serum against the pain that I see now. I think of those lenses that adapt one eye for close-up work and the other for distance. Dizzying.

Why are they so precious to me, why has my threshold for this tenderness dropped so low that seeing a child walk across the room fills me with longing? Perhaps because I want to share, to teach. I have taught, and well, and from time to time praise comes back to me: I am remembered, I influenced. Teaching was a hunger that increased after my own children left home. Now I am being taught, and I love this other side of the golden coin.

In high school, where I barely held my own in some subjects, I was always in awe of my classmate Ben Walter's supple mind. Ben could memorize quickly and speak loquaciously from that memory—or invent to fill in the chinks. "Shovel it on," we used to say. In those years, girls didn't count. We boys could be surpassed in academic matters ("pure memorization," as we scornfully called it), but that's because we saw the girls' lives as so dim and dull that they had time to just sit home and do things by rote. I have little memory of active class discussion involving the girls, but many mental pictures of girls with a hand straining up, bent back at the elbow in that annoying girly loose-jointedness, calmly giving the right answers. How sad, half the humans who were my contemporaries were of another species, to be addressed formally and carefully, in fear that the unmanly act of conversation with one of them might be observed and we'd be teased. On dates, those weekend things, most of the conversation was about how we were really people with similar hopes, but always these were spoken revelations from some other planet, didn't last until Monday, and fostered little sharing during the week. When we were juniors and seniors, things improved. But not, at that time and in my crowd, in serious sexual ways. There could be an increasing companionship on those dates and there was necking, sure. But the yearning, oh the yearning!

Now I imagine myself with these young people as their actual classmate. Aaron would probably be my best friend. I feel at ease with him, and I see us running on overgrown paths to some pond or stream that is our secret place, where we skip stones or make dams. It is summer in this fantasy. I pick him up at his house because we have only one bike, and he rides, gangly, on the handlebars. Sometimes we take a picnic lunch and look up at the sky through leaves as we eat. We walk along perilous cliff edges and climb abandoned water tanks and talk about how scared we are.

Alex I don't know well, but I know him to be a dedicated competitor. I'd want to be on a team with him, and I'd feel honored if he chose me, and I'd say, "Can I play left wing?" or some such, and I'd want his praise at the end of the game.

Mark would be the intellectually daring one, the one we know will be a brilliant professor or politician, and I have an image of taking the train into the city, in midweek, after much hesitation and many phone calls by parents. It is winter, and we wear galoshes and stamp out the thin ice on half-frozen puddles. We are in a group, headed toward a hockey game at the Garden. That's Madison Square Garden, the old one on Eighth Avenue in the Fifties, and we say "at" instead of "in." On the subway Mark stands up and shouts out long quotes from Pliny the Younger to the annoyance of the other passengers, and as I write this now, my skin tingles and recalls to me that the noblest of quests, at that age, was to annoy and bewilder adults. Coming home, we sleep on the Long Island

Railroad, but Mark has brought a Pocket Book, the new invention, and he reads in the jiggling orange pool of light.

Adam is the boy I'd want to be in trouble with. He'd be strong and give me a sideways wink as we stood with heads bowed in front of the constable, and he would have an answer that was meek enough to let us escape prison (which is the fate we fantastically imagine at that age), but his answer is so mysterious or confusing that we are released in despair by the authorities and can remain proud of our caper. The next day he'd tell me what hell he caught from his mom. She, not mine, was called. Mine either never knew what I'd done or blamed it on Adam, who was brave and could shrug it off.

A reason that I would prefer to come forward in time to my classmates and not bring them back to my segregated and sexist past is because I would want to be friends with the girls, plain everyday friends. Sara would be a good friend, she could run with a pack of boys, even to the hockey game, and share her thoughts and give back the teasing, and be handsome and bright but never need "mushy" treatment. What fun to be with her, to be unafraid of girls, be a pal with a girl.

Rachel would be my friend for poetry, and we'd sit under a huge tree and read from cummings or Yeats or Ecclesiastes, or passages from *Look Homeward, Angel* or *The Heart Is a Lonely Hunter.*

With Hannah, I'd want to make things. I'd make tiny furniture for her, an activity that would have disgraced me if I had been caught a half-century ago. Now, I'd pay attention to her lacy small curtains, to where she'd put a piano, and what music she'd want the tiny people to play. I realize now how much strength I'd gain from these girls. Hannah and I made a clay project in our class (we do the full gamut of school stuff, but directed to our purpose). Our clay object is a mezuzah, our book covers are for special notes in religious history, and so forth. Now, after watching Hannah make the delicate petals for a flower decorating the mezuzah, I can't see her without hearing e. e. cummings' beautiful lines, "thy fingers make early flowers of / all things."

Finally, Jami. Our friendship would be the most serious. We would speak, as twelve-year-olds, of the challenges of life, of our hopes for good work, good love, good family. Later in the year, when she became a bas mitzvah, I was the only adult congregant present who was not a relative or invited friend of her family, and therefore Rabbi Doug asked me to present the gift given to each of us at our ceremonies. I stood on the bema and looked into those penetrating, so-dark eyes, and I said to the assembly that if I had to stand up against a mob, that if I had a belief that I was willing to die for and I faced angry thousands, it would be Jami who would stand by me and she would, fearlessly and loyally. Rabbi Doug said afterward that my thought of her was perfect.

Back to school. Could it fail to be, in this personal turmoil— think about it—could it fail to happen, considering all that I've said above, that I could avoid the difficult story that I must tell? Yes, I have a crush on one of the girls. A schoolboy's crush. I am not filled with horror at this; I am not Humbert Humbert and she is not Lolita, I am repelled at that thought. Nor am I some sort of fictionalized Diaghilev, overwhelmed and crumbling in Venice. But I was once dazed and overwhelmed in high school, and now again my schoolboy head turns when this girl comes into the assembly room. These thoughts are not distant echos and reminders of my adolescence, but bring back to me that twinge, the simple need to see that she is in the room. She is not in my class but younger.

She seems a sweet and bright girl. I don't know her, and I hope never to speak to her and perhaps confuse her. Kids are smart in those ways. She's pretty, with a face that is still forming, still blurred and reaching forward to its own pleasant discovery and unveiling two or three years ahead. It is a vulnerable face in that Liv Ullman way, a soft mirror that shows us ourselves. More, the girl who possessed my spirit in high school had that vulnerability, an unfinished feeling to her face, and the similarity is almost frightening to me. There was in that face, now so clearly remembered, a slight nervous mannerism, a mild tic, a blink that hooded her face and whole person for brief infrequent moments, and that is here again, a sudden cloudlike distraction when the features and the life blur and go elsewhere, a visual interruption, and yet it is like a musical tone, like the murmur of a sleeping woman. I do not think I could look straight into the face of this girl, as I could not into the face of the other, those years ago, when I was swept by that first passion.

We so need our flaws. The most beautiful young woman I've ever seen, and Leonora agrees with me, was a dancer we met when I stage-managed and Leonora danced at one of those cabaret weekends at Atlantic City, years ago, before those soft sea-air days died under gambling's wheels. She had a symmetrical and brightly colored face, it doesn't matter and I don't see it clearly now, but what I do remember and still see vividly is a small mole, not protruding, dark and the size of the head of a pin, on her lower lip. Beauty needs that pathway of compassion to draw us in past the wall of veneration. Once I was watching from the wings when the great dancer Eddie Villella fell onstage, awkwardly, like a collapsed wind chime. The audience, the tightly linked other half of a performer, shouted its concern and brought him back again and again for his curtain calls. The lover at last able to do something real for the loved one, able to touch him through a vulnerable spot, like the mole on that beautiful lip. And now, at the annex, this girl stirs an old man like a spoon, as the poet says. Schoolboy indeed!

I do not have a granddaughter who could have been this age, and I'd like so to take this young person to museums, to a ball game, to have seen her wobble off down the street on her first bicycle solo, to hear her squeal at a pretty gift. Those boisterous times with my own daughter passed too swiftly, and like the hull of a boat one's fallen from, they flashed by too suddenly to grasp, too surprisingly soon to have made me realize that I must grasp, and then I saw it going away, and I was alone in the ocean. Now my sight of this reincarnation dims and refocuses, soft dissolves, and I see this young lady at different ages. Is this crazy, Humbert? No and yes. I am stirred, I churn as a boy but without the pain of adolescence: I thought the feeling and the youth were inseparable. She does squeal a lot, this girl, the *"Oh stop it!"* kind of squeal used by girls to comment on boys who are pulling toads out of their mouths and similar ordinary happenings at our school. Squealing distances me from grown women but it is welcome here; it clarifies to me that I am not confusing this girlhood with womanhood.

I don't know if one of these young people in my class could recognize passion as it was for us, and now to speak of that is the only way that I can explain my infatuation and beg understanding for it. I don't beg forgiveness, there's nothing to forgive. Passion was yearning, in those years. It changed so with fulfillment, but that was not to be for years to come, and we accepted and even wanted the delay. We sensed that one cannot go back to days that we knew were precious. Perhaps helped by our fears of inadequacy when the moment should come, we were willing to stretch out our captivity. In those days the world held a reserved seat for us in some imagined arena where there would be space to achieve something of value. If a reserved seat is being held, we don't have to hurry, do we? Do we have, today, this sense of a glowing future? In these instant times do youngsters dare see more than a few years or even months ahead? And yes, they are "sexually active," as the euphemism goes, when they are so young, so that anticipation is gone. Do young people see rewards ahead and are they content to grow toward them? Do even privileged young people today see ahead as I did? It's crowded now, that future.

I wrote a book about stage lighting. In the difficult chapter about "concept," that matrix of time and place and style that pulls together a theater or dance piece, I found one example in a ballet. Anthony Tudor choreographed it, and the clothes were designed by my friend Patricia Zipprodt. A concept of autumn leaves, that sadness, was used in the colors and quality of the set and costumes and lighting. I went further in my chapter and wrote that this was one of the few great themes, perhaps the only great one: growing older and lost love. I've often tried to think of a more powerful theme, or an equal one, but without success.

Growing older, and lost love. I've lost no love in my family, indeed, as that family increases, the love increases, both going and coming. But people fall away, the youthful kinds of love and passion are distant, and the joy and gratitude of having had that love is tempered with its loss. The miracle of our lives is in this subtle and always-moving balance. It can crush you, it can elate you, it can be seen as the great curve of sadness in which we live, not sadness boo-hoo but simply that we must in time step away from this banquet. Melancholy is a sweet mood, often healing, good on an autumn afternoon. I read Chekhov.

We have a friend, ninety now, who said some years ago that just as he was finally at peace with his career, his failures, his sexuality, that just exactly then, "God started taking away my health." Yes, the shifting taut balance of our lives.

I can replay more of my youth now; it warms me and floods me with sweetness. I have a crush, yet another reason to look forward to my classes at the annex.

Chapter 13

☆   ☆   ☆

STUCK HALFWAY

NOTHER DEATH. In November, Landau dies. This was my wife's father, and his death was only a comma in the long sentence that his foolishness and cruelty has imposed on Leonora, and the sentence will continue until her own death. I've not seen her mourn. She struggles with the curse of guilt and anger he put on her when she was a toddler.

No one remembers how long the marriage lasted. Leonora's mother, in one of her Hungarian tell-alls, recounted the many days and nights after the wedding when Landau failed to "end me from being a wirgen." Then he did, but he hung around only a few weeks after the manly success and the impregnation. He was nowhere to be found at Leonora's birth, but the boisterous family surged on with her in tow.

Landau showed up from time to time to scream that he had no money for a doll or a new frock. Leonora, tiny cause and witness to these ugly battles, has never since been able to ask anything for herself. Years later she had some sessions with a psychiatrist, and he talked to me about this deep problem that I was selfishly ignoring. One night she was in real trouble and phoned him to ask for help, and he said that he couldn't see her because he was going away for the weekend. Leonora gently accepted this.

Landau eventually married again, to a woman with money who was so homely that any narrative must pause to seek superlatives. Let me say only that when Nettie came into a room, even the friendly inured could not suppress a gasp: her sudden appearance could cure hiccups. Often she couldn't be touched; she would shriek in pain. One day, twenty years before her death, I heard her scream that she would not have an autopsy. "The huge knives!! The pain, the pain!!" Landau, who couldn't love, linked to a woman who couldn't be touched. But Nettie did have common sense and never lost an opportunity to tell her husband in public that he was a pompous ass. Her nest egg brought him his vocation, and he sat at home and phoned his broker two or three times a day and, surprisingly, increased the fund or, surprisingly, did not diminish it.

For reasons unexplained to this day we would go to their sad apartment on a few Sundays each year. Sometimes, on the way, Leonora would quietly tell me of the beatings from her father, the rapped knuckles at her piano practice during his infrequent visits, or of the time when she was eight that she ran crying into the street, looking for any stranger.

The apartment that we visited was in the center of a confluence of highways out along Queens Boulevard, a vortex of travel, punctuating the fact that Landau and his Nettie never went anywhere. Not quite true. Nettie had inherited a plot of land in Westchester from her Uncle Louie, whom I met only once, when he was over ninety, and I remember his remark that he had never differentiated people by their race or religion or, recently, sex. On that land they built a summer home, roundly cheated by the builder. After ten years they sold it, announcing to Leonora that they were giving it up because we didn't visit them enough. This malignant remark is easily forgiven, because there was one bit of pain they didn't deserve. By bizarre coincidence, the family of Dan's best friend owned the adjacent house, and the Landaus could see their grandchild romping with Josh on many more weekends than they enjoyed him. Dan didn't hate being with Lou and Nettie, but a best friend is a best friend.

In Queens we sat at a half-opened gateleg table jammed into the foyer to convert it to a dining room. Once seated, you had the table pushed against you and there was no way to get out. The rest of the furniture was still in its department-store placenta of plastic, a living room in labor. On one windowsill were three four-inch plastic pots of African Violets, Nettie's hobby. The star turn of the day was the chicken. After an hour of cries, "Is it ready, Lutchell?" (Lutchell must be a Yiddish diminutive of Lou), the bubbling aluminum pot was brought straight to the table and forkfuls of chicken corpse were lifted out, streaming gray fat-frosted water. Up would come the fork, impaling a snot-colored lump of flesh, and then the bone would slide out and gurgle back into the pot, followed by the limp slime-lined skin. There was also something called gravy that followed out of the pot, a yellow transparent afterbirth, or perhaps a boiled jellyfish. I once suggested that Nettie write a cookbook, and she looked modestly down, and Landau stated that he was the cook.

We would sit around after the meal, or after Dan or Julia or both had thrown up, and with the children swinging their legs, Landau would talk about his furniture and the offers he had been made for the various pieces, all under $100. One afternoon he commented on the pipe I was smoking and said that he too had smoked and he would give me his pipe. He hadn't seen it for ten, no, twelve, no—maybe eleven years, eleven. Landau had the habit of repetition of a word or phrase in his sentences, usually not the key phrase. "I believe it's in one of these drawers—one of," he said, going over to an eight-drawer kneehole desk for which he'd been offered $85. He pondered. "Eleven years," he said, and with a magician's bravado he yanked the rotted knob off the third drawer down on the right. When we pried open the drawer, there was the pipe. There was nothing else in the drawer.

After her allotted 85–120 years of justified complaining, Nettie came to her end, swift for her and a week of battle for the rest of us. Sitting down to an evening dinner of chicken leftovers, she said, "Lutchell, something's wrong," and slid off the chair onto the floor (I see her sliding off the fork). Landau sat with her until morning—the doctor shouldn't be disturbed—and when he phoned at nine he was told to call 911. Arriving with Nettie at a Queens hospital, the confused and exhausted old man was asked if he wanted her life saved and of course he said yes, committing us to an unalterable document and a week of excited negotiations with terrified Chinese interns in their own language. Leonora said, "My father mistakenly signed a willing live." Nettie lay brain dead, a nexus of tubes and looking as well as ever. Once this problem was solved there was another hitch, according to my son-in-law, whose Chinese was the best. Nettie had a foot infection, and the hospital could not release her, in either sense of the word, until that was cleared up. So the machine inspired the heart that pumped the blood that healed the infection that gained the release. When the infection improved, the corpse was in acceptable health except for

what had killed it a week earlier. The tubes and pumps were removed and, released, Nettie continued dead but less expensively.
There was no autopsy.

"She was uglier than necessary," said Leonora, exhausted. But I
remember Nettie kindly because of her sallies at Landau.

Landau went into the expected decline and yet he found, even
as he failed, one more way to tear at Leonora's heart. During the
events of Nettie's final days and funeral, a sheep-faced niece made
a strong appearance. Suddenly Landau was full of her virtues. "She
gave up a fifty-thousand-dollar job to raise her daughter. Fifty," he
trumpeted. This relentless theme was soon joined by his declaration that she was so attentive that he was going to leave money to
her, as much as Leonora would get. I talked to him at length, assur-
ing him that leaving money to all of his family was fine, but in this
proportion? I wrote him that he could not ignore the fact that
Leonora had given up the gift of her artistry to raise his own two
grandchildren. He never replied to what I wrote or said. "Fifty
thousand," he tromboned, and Leonora and the rest of us listened
again to the praise. Leonora does not cry. Men cry today, in films
and on TV. Male senators cry. That gives them depth and a rich-
ness as human beings. When women cry, it's weakness.

The niece told us how nice it was that Landau cared about his
whole family, and that she had seen the envelope on which he'd
scribbled the distribution. The day after Landau declared that he
wanted to move ahead with the new will, we received an overnight
letter from her in one of those red-and-white panic envelopes, urging us to use her attorney. I told her that this was her signature act,
thanks a lot, but we'd handle it. The will was made. Landau was
barely capable by that time, but his wish was respected, and it
didn't matter much, because the money was so spread around that

one more toe in the water didn't seriously dilute each person's share. "A brilliant girl, fifty thousand," Landau now said, more quietly, and at the top of my list of those things I cannot forgive is his cruelty in demeaning his daughter. At the end of his life, his last deliberate act was to once again make her feel worthless, to rationalize his guilt and failure as a man who did not nurture her.

Five years later he went on, at the age of ninety-three, in a comfortable nursing home that Leonora found for him. He caused complaint by turning off the "wasteful" common-room lights during card games, and we were phoned each of the three times he decked a Colonel O'Malley, but mostly he continued to be simply boring, loudly announcing his wealth to a dining room full of widows far richer than he.

Said Leonora, "He'll wait until we're on vacation to die. The final straw." He did that. Worn out from theater tensions, we flew to Florida for a long weekend with Peter and Katie Feller. The message awaited us, but we finished the funeral arrangements by phone and stayed for the planned four days. The old Jewish tradition is that Jews should be buried within twenty-four hours, but Landau was not observant. My guess is that he didn't respect his religion because rabbis earn so little.

The old and crowded cemetery was handy to JFK. We drove there in brilliant weather, Leonora commenting on "the clarity of the New York skylight." In a grubby flower shop outside the cemetery, she hesitated between a tired bouquet and a bright GET WELL balloon. A small group met us on the beautiful autumn day. "I'm so sorry," said Cousin Marc as he embraced Leonora. "It's okay, he was old," she said. "No, I mean I'm sorry that I just stood on your foot," said Marc, who had no particular use for Landau, being disinherited because he wasn't interested in women. Landau had almost disinherited Marc's brother Steve because he *was* interested in women and had once "lived in carnal sin. Lived."

The rest of the ceremony was sad and foolish. We had to leave a substantial cash deposit because the papers weren't perfectly in order: faxes, not originals. If faxes are not acceptable in this day and age, how can you bury a Jew in twenty-four hours? If this was the wrong corpse, there would be exhumation expenses. Then we noticed that one of the grave diggers was wearing a black tee shirt, silk-screened with a cascade of what looked like gold coins but were actually skulls. Julia asked if it could be bought at the souvenir shop. At the graveside, Jack spoke well, suggesting that Landau wanted the best for us, and had dandled his grandson Jesse, age two (and screaming), saying, "Young man, you can be anything you want to be!" This brought me up short, because I had recently held a tiny kitten in my hands, trying to not crush it in the surge of passion one has for baby, furry and big-eyed pets, and said, "Sweet kittycat, you can be anything you want to be!" and that struck me immediately as foolish, although it has turned out to be true. When it was my turn to speak, I stepped forward and was overcome with the memory of a nightmarish situation all theater people must face. The curtain has come down on a flop, and you must go backstage and invent lies to tell your friends in the cast. I have no memory of what I said. Finally, the coffin stuck halfway down. Some do-too-much had added side handles, making it too wide for the precise measurements of the graves in these crowded cemeteries. We left him in that state, in the care of he-of-a-thousand-skulls.

And so Landau was off, suspended between heaven and earth,

but the voyage continues in Leonora's heart, restlessly, with sad anger and unexplainable guilt, and no landfall.

. . .

This is disturbing, and I showed this chapter to Rabbi Doug. "Rabbi, one must not speak ill of the dead." His answer surprised me. "Why not?" Then Shakespeare, not Talmud. "'The evil that men do. . . .' David, we do not have to minimize the pain that someone has caused us. Was he repentant?" "No. His last act was vile." Doug's joke, then, tells of the new rabbi who must bury a congregant. The phone starts ringing, a dozen members tell him that the deceased was the worst man who ever lived: a swindler, a liar and womanizer, a wife and child beater. Then a call comes from the deceased's brother. "Rabbi, you have to say something nice about my brother." "But—is there anything nice to say?" "That's your problem. And if you don't say one nice thing, I will withdraw my pledge of $300,000 to the building fund." "But," stammers the rabbi. "No 'buts,' Rabbi. A nice word, or your first act in this congregation will cause $300,000 to disappear!" The next day the rabbi stands over the coffin and says, "Well, at least he was nicer than his brother."

Chapter 14

✳ ✳ ✳

SANTA'S REINDEER

CHRISTMAS NIGHT, returning home after five days in the Catskills. There are miracles that are a part of my story. First, our klezmer band. Our sound is from okay to good, that's not the miracle. The wonder to me is that it started when my life seemed a shambles, when I was fighting to keep that life's work alive, when I was exhausted from the flailings in the lifeboat that would sink us faster than the tempest itself. The call about the band came from Lary Bloom: we'd improvised together on my flute and his piano. "David, we're starting a klezmer band at the synagogue, and you're in it." "Lary, you know I can barely read music and can barely play." "Rehearsal is next Wednesday at eight. See you."

I do not read music well. Herman Commike, our devoted band teacher in high school, would unconsciously hum or whistle the new tunes at my weekly individual lessons. "Here, David, a new

Sousa. Dum dum de-dum-dum, de dum-dum-dum-dum DUM!"
I had a good enough ear to pick up on this, and I believed that I
was reading until I failed band audition at college. I was playing
the baritone horn because when I was fourteen braces were in-
stalled on my teeth and I couldn't produce a sound from the
smaller mouthpiece of the trumpet. Twenty years after my college
failure, I started again, in the musical explosion of the late sixties. I
chose the flute for portability and improvised with my students.
When that blooming of music withered in the seventies, I imagined joining an ensemble to keep up the fun. I went to Pat Harper,
the accomplished teacher of flute at Connecticut College. "Pat, I
can play but I can't read." I tootled for her. "David, you can read,
but you can't play." I took lessons, improved a bit, and now this
phone call—music at last, music out of misery.

I'm the least accomplished in our group. Harvey Redak, forest
ranger and trumpeter, forms professional groups for occasional
gigs. Norman Hanenbaum, sax, and Richard Milgram, clarinet, are
music teachers. Lary plays the keyboard with a ferocity of expression that belies his gentle nature. Jon Joslow, now manager of the
theater company, is a fine drummer who came home unexpectedly
one day and rescued his drum set from a tag sale that his father was
setting out on the lawn. Betsy Kahn plays the hammer dulcimer.
Tim Barry is our bass guitar, not Jewish but married to a Jewish
woman. Our leader is Cookie Segelstein, first chair violist for a
nearby symphony orchestra, but violinist with us. Music joke:
What's the difference between a violin and a viola? If you walk into
a bank with a violin case, they fear it's a machine gun and you'll
take it out and use it. If you walk into a bank with a viola case, they
fear it's a viola and you'll take it out and use it.

Rabbi Doug often joins us on tambourine. Lary has named us

A Klez Act, and we sometimes call ourselves Cookie and Her Klezmer Crumbs, but my favorite is Heavy Shtetl.

Doug says that he thinks that the future of Reform Judaism in America is joy. So be it, this is joy. Of course we talk and argue too much, but we progress. We play fast dances in categories such as Bulgars or Hongas, and slow tunes with names like "Rebbe's Nigun" ("The Rabbi's Tune"), sweet songs such as "Erev Ba" ("Evening Comes"), and some of the sentimental Yiddish songs of the twenties and thirties, such as the waltz "Glik": "Good Fortune, why did you come to me so late? / You give me but a moment of happiness / But I won't think of what tomorrow may bring / As long as we have this brief moment together."

Music was always a miracle to me. Balanchine found the movement for dancers' bodies within it the way Michelangelo found the shape within the stone. For many years I was one of those at Mr. B's right hand as he turned sound to sight, I was a part of his miracle. I was so absorbed in my own theater's disaster that I'd forgotten that blessed life. It's coming back, through our band.

The music is far more than a lift to my own spirits. The entire congregation takes us to heart. We play when we can, and there is usually lively dancing. My favorite is the autumn festival of Simhat Torah, when the Torah reading is finished for the year and the scroll is unrolled and then rewound back to the beginning. One must not touch the lettering of the Torah, so the congregation members line up about three feet apart and gingerly hold the parchment by its top edge. Unrolled, it goes two and one-half times around the small sanctuary space, forming a maze for dancers. The band plays, we all sway, we sing a bit, and when Doug has rerolled the scroll and restored it safely to the Ark, we dance, adults and children. I like to stand near Harvey because the trumpet is loud, so when I'm lost no one will know. Then one night my music stand is knocked down by whirling dancers and I continue anyway. An improvement. By now Cookie has shifted me to piccolo and the good news and bad news are the same: I play it just as well. I play trills, musical spice, and melody only when I feel like it, or can.

There is such a thing as Klezmer Camp, four days in the Catskills at Christmastime. We sign up and drive there. Leonora often closes her eyes as she rides, and often she smiles. When I ask her why, she answers that she is thinking about all of the lovely people we've known who are dead. "Makes me sad," I say. "No, I'm so grateful to have known them." She's right, because if I smile when I think of them as the spirits we walk with now, why shouldn't this extend to smiles at the memory of their lives and skip over the loss? A rider to the BR, the Big Rule.

There is a small miracle, or delight, as we drive. An eighteen-wheeler ahead is obviously down from farther north, because it sports six inches of snow on the trailer's roof. Suddenly the snow layer lifts as one piece, hovers, and descends intact on the car ahead of us. A brilliant white explosion, the car moves on as if it had been through a laundromat. I wish it had landed on us.

The hotel lobby is swarming with kids. The adults, many dressed in colorful Eastern European shirts or vests or caps, are younger than I thought they would be, but it's a mix, with some old bearded guys like me. If you have an interest in this music or culture, why not have your Christmas vacation here? Parents don't have to make the tiresome explanations or apologies on Christmas Day. Many of the little boys wear long tasseled prayer shawls, and the tassels peep out from under the low vests, extending the God part of the boy, the top, and minimizing the beast part, the bottom. The fringes separate the zones.

Klezcamp was started in devotion to klezmer music skills but has expanded to Yiddish culture, from language to dancing to paper cutting, which is not kid stuff, but produces beautiful lacy creations resembling illuminated letters.

Our waitress is full of wisdom. She has some standard jokes: we're nonsectarian here, we hate them all. Indeed, CYO groups and the Knights of Columbus come here. Senior-citizen groups carry them through the winter. In fact, she says, the Jewish clientele is less than 15 percent. Few in the non-Jewish groups seem to mind that the kitchen is kosher. The food is of great variety, and no one would notice an omission except for bacon or ham at breakfast. Rabbi Doug's father-in-law lives near here, so Doug knows the area, and tells me in advance of a good Tex-Mex restaurant down the road, but I don't tire of the food.

So this hotel, begun in about 1908, is surviving. Focus on group needs, good prices, good food and an energetic sales force have kept it alive while dozens of other resorts have closed, including the great Grossinger's nearby. Cars blackened the road in the twenties, thirties and forties, but, says our waitress, the resort business nosedived when Atlantic City gambling opened. I don't agree, I remember an earlier decline when jet travel to Europe and the Caribbean came in. Other reasons may have been air-conditioning, which made New York City bearable in summertime and kept theaters and many other entertainments open. There were polio outbreaks, and we were advised to avoid groups and stay out of the water. Then came the sexual revolution, which made it unnecessary to travel farther than the corner bar to find mates.

Leonora and I met at one of these resorts, Green Mansions. It was farther north than the Catskills, similar to other "adult camps," but famous for its theater. The Group Theatre formed there, and much of our profession can claim that experimental gathering of directors, playwrights, and actors as its progenitor and prototype. When we met, I was the designer, my first professional job. Leonora was a dancer, younger than me but with many gigs behind her. Until now we've never come back to these hills, except for one skiing weekend. It was a dry winter, and Leonora said, "They had to inflict the snow."

We sit at dinner with a filmmaker, Sandy, who is doing a film on "Alternative Lifestyles Among Orthodox Jews." There have been demonstrations in Israel since Prime Minister Netanyahu said that homosexuality is a form of bestiality. In Israel there is a lesbian group calling itself Orthodyke. The men haven't come up with as funny a title. I point out that our rabbi tries to bring gay people into our congregation. He loathes attacks on them, and says, "How dare we oppose whatever happiness anyone can have during their lifetime?"

After our first dinner we go to a staff concert, and I am astonished to see klez greats like Sid Beckerman still here, old now, hanging off his clarinet and playing so well. He makes the instrument laugh and cry and move up scales like a slide whistle. My assigned flute teacher, Marcus Bishko, plays. His group is named the Alaska Klezmer Band, known to friends as The Frozen Chosen. His wife, Victoria, now darts about the stage like Ariel, becoming not only the percussionist (tambourines) but the *tummler,* the person who perks up the crowd with antics, recalling the start in these hills of Danny Kaye and so many others. Marcus' selection is a sweet tune that would be played by groups traveling from house to house at Chanukah. The Chanukah candles were so sacred that one was not supposed to read or write by them—but did a little music hurt? Then Adrienne Cooper sings of Jews in trial, in misery. I'm told that she has the only Yiddish song album that was ever nominated for a Grammy. In the music, this current that carries our history is touching, but I weary of it in the lyrics. Onward! I think of Marianne Williamson's line, "Get off the Cross, we need the wood."

The next morning our flute/piccolo class starts with a simple melody, and Marcus asks us to sing it first. Just "da de, dah de, dah dah," but as you get into it that becomes "a yah, oy yah, oy oy"—yes, you feel the groan of the first six notes, and then you play them, and then you sing the second six, and they are different. The melody lifts and it is full of hope or at least yearning, and these words, after many repetitions, drift, in some places, into the "ah, ah, ah" of yearning instead of "oy, oy, oy" of despair.

After lunch, Leonora takes a dance class, not successful because the teacher talks too much—we've heard that before. The orchestra that I'm assigned to provides the music. I'm crowded in, and the pianist, in front of me, has a baby boy in a backpack, and the child often reaches out and presses keys on my piccolo as I play.

I'm seated behind accordions, which is fun because when we're not playing they occasionally give out a sad sigh, a wheeze, like a whale coming up to blow, or like detumescing bagpipes. When we play, thirty of us, we sound like the Salvation Shtetl Band. The accordionists are instructed that they can play oom-pahs or oom-chucks, and can play either ooms without the pahs or chucks, or the pahs and chucks without the ooms. Music joke: A man is driving home from a gig in the Catskills. He stops for a cup of coffee, leaving his car locked, his accordian in the backseat. When he returns, he sees with dismay that the rear window is smashed. He looks in: there are now *two* accordians in the backseat.

In a series of lectures, Michael Wex talks about Yiddish, that supple, brilliantly colored shrug of a language. He's a riveting lecturer with great phrases—"As useless as cupping a corpse . . ." We learn that to ease the embarrassment of trying to explain the Song of Solomon for cheder boys, the right breast is called Moses and the left Aaron. . . . but any worthy cheder boy can figure it out. Also, there are blessings if a beloved family member or friend dies, but it would be in bad taste to praise the death of an enemy—just the thing the demons wait to hear from you—so you can simply say, "G—d knows what He is doing." His repartee with the class is funny as well: "Did Moses live longer than Methuseleh?" "Lady, you don't know your Gershwin."

Reproductions of Marc Chagall's paintings are much in evidence and explain the spirit of what we are doing. Our days and nights buzz with energy and excitement.

What does this mean to me? Yes, I'm far back in the class, my heritage is just catching up to me. Could I attach to it if I weren't doing something, literally adding a note or a trill? Old village dances and newer Israeli dances move to a beat that I produce and, yes, I join; this is mine. I feel as if a long cloak or train has been pinned to my shoulders.

Christmas night, driving home from Klezcamp, it is overcast, no snow, not cold, almost balmy. Leonora has taken a ride directly to New York City. People are at home tonight, even the roadside McDonald's is closed. There is a sweetness to the countryside and a warmth to the glowing windows: Currier and Ives in the Catskills. I'm ready for an antidote to my klezmer overdose and I turn on the car radio. No sound. Strange, there was a station there. Perhaps a space between events, don't touch the dial yet, and then the miracle, a miracle to me. The great Beethoven Sixth begins. It doesn't start one-two-three-go, it lifts, floats up and gathers, from quietness. A half beat of murmur in the deep strings, then the rising A, B-flat, D. The angel, Beethoven. When I was a little boy, I remember walking with my mother and another woman, and I must have been small because I was holding Mom's hand, and the other woman said, "Ah, but where would we be without Mozart?" Mozart, Beethoven, Bach, fill in your own blanks. How could a small child remember that conversation? Because I made a game of the strange name, "Mo Tzart, Mo Tzart, Mo Tzart, break your heart," and worse, later. You know the way kids practice sounds, finding that strange man who lived in the middle of the alphabet, Ellemenno Pee.

It wouldn't have been a miracle if I'd deliberately put on my own cassette but I hadn't, and from stillness the melody gathered and rose in the quiet night. It was after the storm in the music, when that cloud-clearing bridge is made by the clarinets and horns, then the flutes, and then sunlight breaks through on the first violins, and I was floating on the straight highway, Interstate 84 west of the Hudson, when a deer ran into me, destroying his life (and the left side of my car). *Bang!* The sound alone of the flying metal crushing him, the solidity and finality of the accompanying *thunk,* allowed no thought of survival. I saw or knew, I can't remember which, that he lay off the road, and when I drove back to the scene with a state trooper, we found first the shattered glass and metal bits of my left headlight, then a dark pool of blood at the road's edge, then the body of the large buck just beyond that in the grass.

Do we die instantly? Isn't there a fraction of a second left to us? At fifty-five miles per hour, say eighty feet per second, isn't that about a sixteenth of a second for the stag to be hit and move the five feet down the hood of my car to the windshield? Longer, surely, because the impact moved him forward with the car, but I know that he was alive when I looked directly into his huge brown eye as his head came to the windshield, two feet in front of my own eyes. Then he was by, gone, and then after a separate tiny gulf of silence, I heard and saw and felt a thousand fragments of glass, the driver's-side window, settle and glitter on my shoulder and lap. Christmas decorations.

In far less than a second, one by one: the solid impact and realization, the great eye, alive but in its last instant of life, the silence, the glass. Then the cold flowing in where the window had been, then Beethoven surging again into the darkness. I see the eye now, recognizing its warmth and great size and beauty, because we give beauty to animals that resemble our species. I try to imagine images of skulls, skeletal bones, and gaping mouths in that lens in the instant that it flashed by, but I only remember the size and the brown warmth of the eye. I was not afraid, it was not the kind of situation that flaps me: I can lose my cool at a board meeting but not during an accident. Nor did the stag seem afraid or shocked or panicked, as I had seen a year before when a deer ran into the same side of the car, but then I was driving slowly down the winding road into my town, and the deer wasn't running fast and was unhurt.

In my memory now the live eye of the animal was a full mirror, the absolute center of the flashing scene, and the sense of death was huge and personal. Eyes mirror us everywhere in our paintings, in the magnificent mosaics at Ravenna, in the eyes of the statues of antiquity, once polychromed but now faded, looking at us from the essence of time and death. The lead statement in the proclamation of justice in the Torah's Book of Exodus is "an eye for an eye," citing the part of us that we understand as soul—and I'm sure that's what it means, not literally "eye." The eye most haunting to me is the eye of a sea beast, a monstrous devilfish that fishermen pull onto the beach at the end of Fellini's film *La Dolce Vita*. Fellini gave us enigmatic symbols that stay and stay, like the great ship passing in *Amarcord*. In *Dolce Vita*, in an ashy dawn after a night of shallow play, the drained jet-set partygoers run to the beach to look into the sightless eye of the monster dredged from the deep. Again water, perhaps containing in horrible darkness forms of life that we can't imagine. The monster, alive, would be a dumb beast. Dead or dying, in Fellini's haunting context, we see death in reverse. Just so with the stag: death looks at us.

Chapter 15

*   *   *

THE EXPLODING CHICKEN

WE HAVE AN ICE STORM. These were my mother's favorite outbursts of nature and they caused the only times she ever phoned me. I always phoned her, almost every day. But perhaps once each winter she would phone me, so excited. "Have you looked out the window? Have you seen?" She didn't even care if her precious branches were breaking. The ice on the branches glittered and the air was shining with diamonds, the air became diamonds, swaying and glittering; you couldn't even look at them when the sun was behind them. "It's a miracle!" she would say, and that's as far as she went, God enough for her. An ice storm is impressive, I wonder at it and am touched and moved. Better than walking on water. The water walks onto the trees and branches and transforms the trees, miracles themselves, into a holy brilliance.

I've been in the miracle, well, the magic business. That's what theater design is supposed to do, once in a while. I enjoy the magic that, like the ice storms, can be explained yet catches you by surprise and whips up your spirit. I enjoy the glorious things we know everyday, transformed. Ice storms.

We try to create delight. I worship the human imagination; worship is too strong a word, but not by much. Every so often it comes at us with whirlwind force: Balanchine, Stravinsky. But it also happens on a smaller scale, and these are precious happenings. The Theatre of the Deaf did a production based on the film *The King of Hearts*. A fine, fine director, J Ranelli (yes, J without the dot), created it with the company, and a fine, fine deaf actor and painter, Chuck Baird, painted the scenery on paper panels as the show progressed—match that! At one moment in act two—a World War One battlefield was the place—a shell was to land and explode. Not difficult, stage detonations are easy. But should a touring company put its presenters through the tedious and uncertain process of getting the permit? Just for one small bomb, no pun intended? Not if there's a more amusing way to do this. Just before the moment our stage manager, Fred Noel, who was in evidence anyway, bringing on the fresh paper panels for Chuck, pushed a pole onstage. At its onstage end was a nest with a hen sitting on it. The hen was made the way Matthew and I made that bird for Sukkot, but instead of pasting paper wings on a blown-out egg, we put them on a blown-up balloon about the size of a football. The wings and beak and comb of the hen, all cut from stiff colored paper, rested on the balloon. The shell approaches, we hear the descending whistle and, for the sake of the deaf (which is why farts smell), the cast apparently spots the "incoming" and follows its imagined arc down to the chicken, which exactly then explodes, pierced by a thrust of a pin at the end of the pole. *Bang!* A bull's-eye, the chicken blown right out of the nest by the nasty bomb!

The wings and beak and comb fly up and flop on the stage nearby. Laughter, applause, surprise and delight. Obvious magic, you can see how it worked.

Our Wednesday class begins with the short service, and today Doug includes a prayer for Ben's teacher, a Mrs. Hamilton, to give her patience and strength. In the classroom I look at the map tacked to the wall. These kids aren't good at the geography of Europe, or of anyplace. They can't figure out where this and that country is without their computer programs, and they may need calculators to add two and two, but so do the grocers, who can no longer add four-figure numbers rapidly down a brown paper bag. I'm worse than the kids because I don't care much about geography and addition. I look at a map and I see only water, and the ports—and miracles. Water again brings me back to miracles, to the fog wall that can split our river Thames as crisply as a concrete wall; boats suddenly and magically materialize and, above, a decorative cornice of cloud divides the curtain-wall from the blue sky. Pfizer's chimneys and a yellow crane from Electric Boat Company come and go halfway up.

On the 21st of March, during Friday evening services, after his announcement that the Holy Scrollers (our Bible study group) will tomorrow read of animal sacrifices at the start of Leviticus, Doug speaks directly to me from the pulpit. Might be a good disciplinary idea for his Hebrew class, he says. Do I agree? "Eat your heart out, Doug," I say, which in retrospect seems a poor, unintended, pun.

Leviticus, book of sacrifice techniques and skin diseases, also has some elegant passages such as "Love thy neighbor as thyself." So what if there are twenty-odd pages of instruction on skin diseases and how to behave? If my mother had written them there would be forty. Doug says that when he was a student, each year his synagogue invited a dermatologist to comment on the skin passages, and after the comments he would hand out his card.

Leviticus is at the middle of the five books, and it's the only one where the tribe stays put, entirely at Mount Sinai. In the old tradition, this was the book of Torah that was taught first, and in the old libraries, if there could be only two books, the first would be the Torah and the second the Sifra, which is the rabbinic commentary (midrash) on Leviticus. This is the book that tells us how to approach and deal with God. Remember that God entered the tent: He was there with them. Of course there is no firm evidence that the Tabernacle, so exactly described, was really built. Maybe they had a building committee like ours.

We learn that the high priests could not go into the tent where God lived if they had physical imperfections. This is in Leviticus 21 and is repeated later. Among the imperfect are those with a broken arm, a hunchback or dwarf, one who is spotted in the eye or with crushed testicles. Ow! "Doug," I ask, "was that so common to be that high on this list? It's not an everyday cause of distress today, in my circles, anyway." Doug agrees but remembers a passage from James Dickey's *Deliverance* that notes how farmers, and those were farmers in Leviticus, are so often bunged up: fingers gone, bodies broken and sprained by some piece of equipment or animal. I find the passage at our library: "I never saw a farmer who didn't have something wrong with him . . . The work with the hands must be fantastically dangerous . . . the catching of an arm in a tractor part . . . domestic animals turning and crushing one against the splintering side of a barn stall." The moral of all of this, I later pose to Doug, is that when you beat your swords into plowshares they will whip around and smash you in the nuts. That's my grandson Jesse's word. "Genitals," his father corrects him. "Yeah, balls," says little Jordan.

Doug speaks of what the great skies brought to the farmer. I am an expert on the fright of this immensity as seen from our diminutive boat, our progress too meager to evade the majestic and menacing advance toward us. At sea there is no storm cellar to hide in and the consequence is immediate—not watching the crop slowly wither, but being swallowed alive. Of course the comparison doesn't hold up, there are deadly hurricanes and twisters and fires ashore, but think about seeing that sky, horizon to horizon, hour after hour of watching it, straining to see menacing signs at sundown, then watching stars snapped off one by one by the approaching sheet of black.

When I was a boy I would often squat by a mud puddle and find a bubble and imagine that there was an entire universe, as big as ours, inside that bubble, and perhaps our universe was in a bubble in another, bigger puddle. Did I, as a child, believe in God? Of course I did. I had been told of Him and that was that. Then something happened. Proust, in *Remembrance of Things Past*:

> As I grow older, and life becomes more quiet around
> me, I hear again the sound of the sobs that I could al-
> ways control in the presence of my father, but which
> burst from me when I was alone with Mother. It's not
> as if their echo ever ceased—no—it's as if the morning
> bells of the convent were so consumed by the bustle
> and noise of mid-day that one might think they had
> ceased forever—until they ring out again clearly in the
> quiet evening air.

My autumn leaves, Mom's sunsets and the clear ring of the God I did not question as a child is coming back, or let me say that

I'm searching for Him now, in this quieter time. I don't look at bubbles in puddles, but just the other day, in an unexpected glow of warmth before the next season, before winter returned as the ice storm, I lay on my stomach in my backyard, so much less secure than when I used to do this in my parents' yard; I lay there and stared at a one-inch square where moss joins grass. I looked for tiny teeming life, and that has always been my way of understanding the hugeness of the universe.

Back to school. We learn that in the prayer *M'chayey Ha-Metim*, where the dead will come back to life, that word *metim*, (dead), is translated as "all things." This is because about one hundred years ago Reform Jews decided that resurrection was pie in the sky. In our tradition, the Messiah will come someday, led by Elijah. Then we address Jami's point that she doesn't believe in God because she doesn't see him. Mark says you do see him, in everything—walls, chairs, and so forth, but I'm not sure that Mark has any more grip on God than she does, or I have, for that matter. She asks why God gave us the Commandments if he knew we'd break or ignore them? Doug says that those who love us make rules for us, and he shapes this into his opinion that the kids revolt against God as a part of their revolt against their parents. The kids agree that, yes, there could be a connection. Jami comes back to her point, a sense of oppression, taxation without representation, she feels. She doesn't believe in God, and yet He oppresses her with His rules. And if He loved us so, how could He permit the Holocaust?

I do well on my prayers, and Doug is pleased. How much of my haftorah will I do? Not all, maybe, says Doug—I say that's good, because I'll do it slowly and bore people. So, says Doug, where else do they have to go on the Sabbath? To lunch, I say, but he seems unmoved by that, so I craftily shift my argument, "I mean I maybe

can't learn it all," and he laughs. "And give me time," I say as I recite, "Don't jump in to correct me too quickly! Besides which, your
shirt has crabs (it's a Maryland tee shirt) and they're *trayf.*" But I
don't say "Shush up, Rabbi!" like one of my classmates—you can
guess who by now—when he jumps in too fast.

The old Isaiah isn't the Isaiah who wrote my passage, says
Doug. This writer was later, perhaps living in Babylonia during the
exile. Could the references to light and restoration mean going
back to Jerusalem to build the second temple? Perhaps this was
written after the first temple was destroyed, and Isaiah is saying
don't give up hope, we will rise again. Doug does not believe that
these passages prefigure Jesus. "It's the subject—" I start, and Doug
completes the sentence, "—of much Christian discussion."

In our next meeting, Jami is full of noes, but the class is peaceful. Adam, Mark and Sara are absent. So is my heart-lifting girl—
this is school vacation week. We comment on the list of *verbotens*
for Jews in Nazi Germany in the thirties—how they would affect
us. "Do I have to read," asks Jami? "Yes, you do," says Debbie, and
Jami does, beautifully. Later she says, "My hand hurts, I can't write
more." Of course she doesn't expect this to be taken seriously, but
that's not the point. With these kids the noes are an art form. I'm
sure that there's been much rabbinical discussion on that.

The next hurdle is dancing. A light-footed, an Astaire-footed,
instructor leads us. I try to sit most of it out, but when Jami refuses
to dance, my clear duty is to lurch up to the ring of waiting dancers
and say, "C'mon, Jami, you can't be the only one not dancing," and
I grab her hand and pull her to the circle, and so I suffer for that. I
never could dance, and now that I can barely see my feet it's worse.

My mother never showed an ounce of religious feeling, neither
did Dad. Ethnic feeling? Zionism? Hadassah? United Jewish Ap-

peal? The kind of spiritual feeling that kids want from their parents? Yes to all, yes indeed. All of this is covered in our class workbook, where types of Jews are listed, ranging from the Orthodox, who wish no laws to be changed, to Reform Jews, who wish change and their choice of which traditions to keep. Then there is Jewish Secularism, where you are Jewish without being religious; and a confusing variation of this, where I place my family and many friends, is called Reconstructionism, whose adherents believe we should practice the religious customs that keep the Jewish people united and the Jewish civilization alive. Mom might go for that. She worried, for example, that Jews might join country clubs and start to drink, perish the thought. Might Jewish students no longer be at the top of the honor rolls at colleges if we outgrew the scrutiny of prejudice? Good call, Mom.

Dad never told me his religious feelings. He worked on various councils toward interfaith understanding and was effective. He became president of Temple Israel in Lawrence, Long Island, a beautiful and large Reform temple—so "reformed" that the boys in the Conservative temple teased us for going to a church. But a leader and a fund-raiser doesn't have to know a prayer, and Dad did not. Worse, he'd fall asleep on the bema Friday nights. That's how our good deed began.

In 1938, Dad went for a weekend sail with his cousin Edward Nathan. He liked it. My brother went with him. I was only eight, distracted somehow and only dimly aware that I had missed an adventure that was described in terms of bumped noggins and damp berths. But Dad was hooked and thought that this was the way to raise his boys. So a boat was bought, a big and comfortable boat, sixty feet long, the schooner *Sunbeam*, designed by John Alden.

With it came a captain and a cook. Not bad. I never thought of us as rich, and that was probably Mom's doing, but Dad was a fine lawyer who had not lost money during the Depression, and a boat of that size could be bought for under $10,000 at that time. The crew salaries—and these were family men—were $35.00 per week.

Why didn't Mom yell at Dad for buying a boat? Everyone's always yelled at me for doing nothing worse than that, and one of the ironic twists of my life is that finally, after spending a fortune on boats, I earned it all back with the book that Dan and I wrote about a voyage, and perhaps my son has a vocation in his fine writing. But Mom—why did this woman, who described polo as, "Humph, games from the top of a horse," a horse being what a Cossack rides into the shtetl the faster to kill you—why did she accept a boat, a *yacht* no less? Partly because she was mortified when Dad fell asleep on the bema, which was partly caused by a dull rabbi, and partly because the dull rabbi's wife, campaigning to keep her husband from being fired, was a constant pest in our home. Mom wanted to end all of that. So Dad resigned from the temple and we went sailing. We would go to the boat just after school let out in early June, and that included Mom, which hadn't been in Dad's initial plans. We sailed all summer and came home on Labor Day. When, periodically during the summer, Dad went in to the city to work, he'd leave the boat with the captain in charge of our safety and Mom in charge of him. We'd be at anchor in an active harbor, such as Newport or Marblehead. Richard and I would madly sail the dinghy or play with friends we made ashore, such as the son of the New York Yacht Club steward, in Newport.

Dad's law partner Herman Shulman had a son Paul, about four years older than my brother, who sailed with us. He was husky and skilled and cheerful, and he also fell in love with the water. He went to Annapolis, and after serving at sea in the Second World War he went to Israel and became the brilliant admiral of their tiny navy. An Egyptian destroyer was sunk in Israel's first war for survival in 1948, and the seas were made safe for the new country. That's how, starting with my dad's snoring during Friday night services, my family saved Israel.

Milton Handler, a lawyer and law professor whom my Dad admired and vice versa, told me a story about this when he was ninety-two. We were at lunch at his elegant club, the Harmony Club, created in 1852 by German Jews and kept for many years, said Milton with a smile, as a bastion against the newly arrived Russian Jews. During that 1948 Arab-Israeli conflict, said Milton, there would be frequent councils of war. Things were going well enough for Israel, and at one meeting David Ben-Gurion, after getting the reports from his chiefs, turned to Paul. "Shulman," he said, "what do you need?" "Prime Minister," said Paul, "I want a submarine." Ben-Gurion turned to his chief of staff and asked, "So how much costs a submarine?" "David," was the answer, "your parents were *schneiders,* my parents were *schneiders,* he wants a submarine, we'll get him a submarine." A *schneider* is a tailor, and among its other meanings is "someone who lives by his wits."

April 2nd, in class. Mark wants to say the Kaddish, the prayer for the dead, at services. Doug says no, an unusually firm no, and the matter is dropped. Later I ask him why. Is Mark too young, before bar mitzvah? Is saying this prayer the rabbi's unique duty? Doug says, with humor, that some come from a Reform tradition, some from an Orthodox tradition, some from a tradition of superstition. Whatever the mix, he says, I don't want a young person whose parents are still alive to say that prayer. The angels, you know, might find a reason to justify his recitation.

In my lesson after class, I crash totally on my haftorah. I tell Doug that I've become top-heavy and I can't seem to stuff any more in my brain, critical mass and all that, and my effort to do so has dislodged what was there and all has gotten "out of shape." That's a phrase born on the river. When St. Louis (water transport) and Chicago (rail transport) were competing, the rail companies built their bridges across the big rivers with piers at angles to the flow of the water. When the tugs pushed their loads in strong current through these angled gaps, the string of barges got "out of shape," and it was a tedious task to line them up again. Riverboat or not, Rabbi Doug seems relaxed about my dilemma.

Sara's lesson follows mine. "Why are we sitting out here, Rabbi?" Anything to not settle down to work. She's not in trouble, I reflect gloomily. I chat with her mother, who gives me useful catering advice for my bar mitzvah party.

We're to have a short Seder in school, and we start by making designs with crayons on a long and narrow paper tablecloth. My idea is the best! The edges of the tablecloth will be waves, and in between them, along the length, each of us will draw a group of walking-running figures—the Israelites escaping on the dry land between the waves. Then the waves can close in to the center and we can draw Egyptians swimming, or worse. It goes well, but Adam writes STAR WARS and makes stars and rocket ships attacking the cloth. He *is* bored with all of this.

Then the whole school sits at tables covered with our tablecloths, and parents have brought food—the ceremonial parts, anyway. Doug wears a backpack. "Why am I wearing this?" he asks.

"Because you're leaving Egypt." "Right. And what am I taking?" "Video games!" cries a small child. Doug wears his white coat, symbolizing goodness.

My crush, my Young Lady, is there, acting silly and giggly like any twelve-year-old, squeaking out "Oh *stop* it" to some boy showing off—all the stuff one should expect. And what did I expect? That she should soar heavenward into the blue sky with the laundry, like Remedios the Beauty?

On the 24th and 25th of April, Leonora and I take Jesse and Jordan to Washington, D.C., and it's a classic grandparents trip. On the way down, on Amtrak, we don't have seats in the short string of cars put on for this holiday weekend. Amtrak is delightful, each day dawns fresh and new; no experiences from the past taint them. Also, I treasure their explanations. Example: Me (to stationmaster at Penn Station, some years ago): "Why is the escalator going down when the train has just discharged passengers and we all have to go up?" Stationmaster (astonished, to me): "Buddy, do you know how hard it is for people with emphysema to walk down stairs?" In our car there is a large empty space where seats might have been, and that suits the kids—it's like an open playground. There is another boy their age, and we learn everything we have to know about cheek popping, flower tongue, head thumping, toilet peeking, toilet-door locking, baggage-rack chinning, aisle wresting, plastic-wrapper blowing, paper-plate stomping, ghost woo-wooing, jaw wah-wahing, greasy-palm window staining, up-skirt observing, and we learn about farting sounds made by the palm of one or both hands held over the mouth just so, or made the old-fashioned way, which even I can do, the mouth on the forearm, and also by the hand-in-the-flapping armpit method. These sounds are most effective, we learn later, when an inconspicuous small person, say seven or nine years old, stands at the edge of the sidewalk and makes these sounds as a group passes by. Points are awarded based on how many heads turn to look at others in the group, and whether the speaker pauses.

We go to the Smithsonian to see the great machines and cars and carriages and ship models, and where you watch the pendulum. Management has granted much space to computer devices, and kids enjoy the screens and "interact," the current word. The magnificent carriages and cars don't fascinate them as they did me. Perhaps they've seen them on videos, with skillful explanations, and of course the carriages are in motion on the screen and drawn by gorgeous horses, complete with the sound of hoofbeats and the sight of swirling dust and an engulfing musical score. I might have seen such images as a child—on film of course—but I would have gasped to see *The Real Thing*. Now computer screens are the real thing.

We have supper at a seafood restaurant that is, according to Leonora, along the Pontiac. More hot dogs the next day. Then home on the train the next morning, and the kids are tired but involved in a book, *Freddie the Detective*, a favorite of mine as a kid, and my grandfather-crankiness about progress is slightly mollified.

Bel Kaufman comes to us on the next Sunday, for our morning "Books and Bagels," and my planning as a member of our program committee pays off. Doug says that the three books on his grandmother's bookshelf were the Bible, plus Sholom Aleichem, plus Bel's *Up the Down Staircase*. One for God, two for the Rabinowitz family, says Bel. I say that Bel isn't that old; next we'll hear that her book was found in the Second Temple. The Hormone Hurricanes are there, excused from class to hear Bel, and they demonstrate, probably to tease Doug, that they can be attentive. Bel speaks of her grandfather, Sholom Aleichem, a kindly man whose lifetime ended in the Bronx. She speaks of our backgrounds—who we are now is so much what we were. She says that she loves our fresh, Jewish faces, not realizing that this congregation, as humorously claimed by Lary, is only 48 percent Jewish.

"Laugh anyway," says Bel. "You'll get the joke later."

Chapter 16

*   *   *

SAYING JESUS, OFFSHORE

W E GO TO EXUMA, in the Bahamas, for the Christmas–New Year's stretch. Leonora says, "It's a third-war country."

Amazelle, a woman of my age who comes to us to clean and to cook tasty meals, invites us to her church, the Church of the God of Prophets. This is in her settlement of a dozen one-story homes. Hers is coral colored and neat and pretty. My daughter-in-law-to-be, Wendy, and I have accepted the invitation, and we enter at 11:30, at the end of Sunday school, in time to hear the blessing on the school and students. All the young people and adults stay on for the service. We are in a simple white-painted, low-ceiling room, but the ceiling is gently arched, which makes the room airy and comfortable. There is a center aisle, and the wooden pews could hold perhaps two hundred worshippers, but we learn later that there are only eight member families. About twenty scrubbed youngsters and fifteen women are scattered in the pews in the front half of the room, and the women, of all ages, are beautiful in flowered cotton dresses with long or half sleeves. All wear hats—a flower garden. There are only four men: Pastor Christopher Ferguson, who is Amazelle's husband; the deacon, a younger man who will read parts of the service and stage-manage the comings and goings to the small lectern; and two musicians: the organist and another who plays the electric guitar. The organ is a small electric keyboard with an organ stop.

We start with a "PRAISE THE LORD," and the band starts. The organ hints at melody, and there is a sense of bass beat from the guitar. There is also a drum section, and what carries the band, now an enormous sound in the vibrating room, is a boy who is eleven (I learn later from Amazelle) in a white shirt with flowing Russian sleeves. He is on the snare. Can he knock that drum! The snares snarl and the beat jumps, driving and swift. Now the room is pulsing and swaying, flowers in a breeze. The bass drum is whacked by a smaller boy, six, and he is steady as what, a church? Loud and fast, *Boom! Boom! Boom!* The cymbals are stroked together, no clashes, which is the only disappointing touch. The player is a girl who is the sister of the snare drummer. She is taller and looks older, but is actually younger.

We sing familiar hymns, and I try to read the shaped notes in the hymnal. We don't always get the title but we pick up the tune, and even with the racket we hear a word now and then. *Boom! Boom!* the beat is steady and sometimes the bass drum syncopates, it is tireless and leaping with energy. We sing, at the tops of our voices, "Hand in Hand with Jesus," "Jesus Walks with Me," "Victory in Jesus," "I'll Fly Away," and a dozen other hymns with names that I didn't quite catch, and there is a Christmas carol thrown in. Did I really shout out "PRAISE JESUS?" After the first hymn, the deacon invites groups of women to the pulpit, and each speaks a few words of faith with driving enthusiasm and then leads a hymn. The clapping is often an intricate pattern of claps and handshapes.

"Is this the way your church works at home?" I ask Wendy, who is glowing even more than usual and so am I, I know. "No, we're sedate, the hymns are sung, not belted out, we have a choir. Paler stuff."

Now the tiny bass drummer has exchanged his padded club for the cymbals. Then I see him taking a rest, sitting beside the snare drummer and gazing at him with his huge and brilliant black eyes. An adoration, right here in church. After the service he must surely say, "You're an inspiration to me, Bix." Now, five rows back, a young woman produces a tambourine, and her long-fingered graceful hand races over it as swiftly as a harpist's at full speed.

Understand that this drumbeat, snare and bass, drives the hymns at breathtaking speed: they streak around the rhythmic corners on two wheels. They are all marches, no exceptions, including the carol, rat-a-tat-tatted, pounded, with snares buzzing and an occasional rim shot. Try it sometime—"Silent Night" to a fast march beat.

Finally the basket is passed, and I put in two dollars—too much. Then we have the sermon, and a rattler it is. Preacher Ferguson wears a thin, dazzling, Chinese-red tie. He doesn't need the microphone. His voice soars and expands and stays there, and I wonder if it can last the sermon. He begins gently enough, asking us to join him in a prayer for the sick and the evicted. We do that at home, the sick anyway. I presume that Connecticut Jews aren't evicted enough to call for sanctified recognition. The sermon is based on the Twenty-third Psalm, and Pastor Ferguson goes line by line through this beautiful poem. He takes a line and explains it:

sheep cannot drink at rough water, and even the River Jordan can be rough, so the Lord makes a ditch to a quiet pool where they can drink. The green pastures—just look out these windows into our paradise on earth. It all makes beautiful sense and is so accessible. The delivery, at top volume yet well inflected, is filled with joy and glory. The Reverend sometimes steps right up into air, or so it seems. Of course he is only jumping with excitement, but there may be real if brief levitation. The congregation is attentive, swaying and affirming with cries of "Yes! Amen!" and an occasional "Hallelujah!" The preacher's final theme is that we've just finished one year, this is the first meeting of the new year, and Jesus was with us last year, don't you know He'll be here in this next year?

After the sermon, there is another prayer, again for the sick and also for those in jail. It's hard to imagine anyone on this island paradise spending much time in jail, but Pastor Ferguson may include all the black brothers who do time, wherever they are. The only men I personally know in the slammer are Ravenal and our synagogue's former treasurer, who embezzled us back home, and we don't pray for them. Also, at home, we say prayers for the dead, but here in Exuma this is not strongly stated; the dead are not addressed with finality. They may not lie quietly, but dance in an even lovelier place to a celestial snare drum.

We leave after the sermon and a few short prayers, and the announcements for the week, delivered by Amazelle. She includes a gracious thank-you to us for attending. I know that guests are welcome and recognized in most churches and synagogues, but this is sad and hurts because I sense that we are white people, being thanked for just paying a bit of attention. We forego the foot washing; that seems too personal for visitors to join.

Wendy and I, like the church we are leaving, are jumping with

excitement. I don't even try my prepared line, "I missed the Hebrew." I tell Wendy that my old God can help me, but I'll have to
walk with him, he won't just lead me. I'll take my responsibility
and understand myself and Him better, but I doubt if I can hand it
all over to him, as the Reverend asks me to hand over all of my
troubles to Jesus.

But I've made a friend, and this small step is meaningful to me
on my tiny pilgrimage. A friend, or at least I am finally comfortable
with an old, an old what? Not an enemy; I have understood that Jesus spoke as a Jew to other Jews. But I've been told in no uncertain
terms that I'm His enemy; I've been told that I killed Him. I hate
that; can't I feel at ease with the Jesus who inspired such brilliant
art, such music? This is one reason why, in my studies and thinking, I must have been heading toward the relief of whatever it is,
deeply ingrained, that has made me wince at Jesus' name when I
occasionally say it. This inner wince, however slight, is also a reflex
in most other Jews I've asked. Being called (yelled at, when we were
kids) "Christ-killer" is the most frequently stated cause. There are
other reasons, less easily stated: a sense of exclusion, the notion
that dawns on our children that the gentiles have the new, the best
thing, that we missed the boat, missed lavish Christmases and that
flood of holiday spirit and the carols that everyone else seems to be
singing. We just didn't stay tuned, there is a whole maxi-series after
the Old Testament. The name "Jesus," thrown at us, is the invisible
line drawn. Leonora doesn't know where her wince came from, but
she says it's there. Recall the day when you were twelve, reading
aloud in class, and there was a word like "intercourse" and you had
to say it. As Leonora says, "It made me scringe."

I'm making progress. At a party I meet a lawyer with beautiful
eyes. She is a born-again and surprises me with her liberal views.

Yes, the fundamentalists get the press, the abortion clinic shoot-'em-ups get confused with all of this. Her position is simple. She reads the Bible, Old and New Testaments, with no intermediary. She believes what she reads, but not always literally. She can accept some of it as legend created from experience and wisdom and inspiration. Her new faith (she was raised as a Catholic) began when she was in a severe automobile accident and lay in a coma. She had a white-tunnel experience, an experience of dazzling light and warmth and kindness and beauty. I've read about many such experiences and doubted them, but I believe her, for the first time I believe this. Another layer peeling away from me? She believes in Jesus, but she has no problem with my older, solo God, and she believes that faith is faith, and the system expressing it is secondary. She believes in the afterlife, and I don't feel uncomfortable. She mentions a symbol used by believers like herself, a small metal fish design attached on her car. I've noticed these but thought that they were some symbol of the dealer. No, it's Christian. "If you crash into another car with a fish," I ask, "does that driver rush out and yell 'Fuck thee!'?" and she laughs.

Until we moved to Connecticut when I was eleven, my best friend was the boy next door. We played every day after our different schools, until we were dragged in to supper. His parents were attentive to me, and I once asked my mother why we never invited them to our house for dinner, and why they never asked us. She didn't answer in words, but the way she turned from me was a warning to never ask again. Then one day Mickey and I had a squabble, I can't remember the topic, but it was in his room. He called me that name, "Christ-killer," and I didn't even realize that it was important until he repeated it in front of his mother as I fled through the kitchen. She did not disapprove. I didn't tell Mom, I knew from the way she had turned that she would step in, that there would be a war and that I would lose my friend forever. I didn't know enough to understand the insult and I was already, along with Mickey I'm sure, inventing ways to pick up our friendship the next day, which we did. With time, after we'd moved away, I understood, and now I'm sorry that he carried around that baggage, that ready ammunition, surely loaded on him at his parents' table and ready for emergency use. The good news, of course, is that in 1964 the Pope declared that Catholics shouldn't blame the Jews for the killing of Jesus. Twenty-four years too late for me and Mickey, almost two thousand years too late for many, many others, but thanks anyway, Pope. "Humpf," Mom would say.

Mom wasn't a bigot, she was a woman under siege about almost everything, and she was defensive about the world her children would live in. After the Holocaust she was concerned about our living on as a people. There was little religion in our home, but there was passion for our people and for Zionism.

She had the usual wince for the name "Jesus Christ," but it didn't come up often. Once I saw her bruised. Her granddaughter, my niece, had been raised as a Presbyterian. When she was married in a formal church ceremony in Greenwich, the minister used the phrase "Our Lord Jesus Christ," a thousand times, or so it seemed. Each repetition hit Mom like a burst of machine-gun fire but she had no thought of retreat, and with Julia holding her on the right and my own arm-grip on her left side, she swayed back to bolt upright after each blast. The insensitive or merely unwarned minister might have kept the glory turned down to the usual dosage. But the religion chosen for those grandchildren, my two nephews and two nieces, never stopped Mom from giving them as much love and concern as she gave to her Jewish grandchildren on my side.

Now the world has gone around a bit; I'm full of delight to spend this time with an adorable young woman who was slated, all of those searching years, for my son. Thanks a *bissel* to her, thanks a *bissel* to Pastor Ferguson and to the lawyer with beautiful eyes, I'll be able to say "Jesus Christ" with ease, now my friend if not my God.

In any case, there can be no question that Exuma needs an old Jewish piccolo player, and I'd love to play in that band.

Chapter 17

* * *

MY REPORT CARD

WET CEMENT! There is a new path to the front door of the synagogue, and a mason is finishing the final trowel strokes. Instead of simply digging the narrow ten-foot walkway by hand, a backhoe was brought in, and that tore up the front yard, so a truckload of topsoil was needed, then a steamroller came to level it. The mason hears my complaint, laughs, collects his tools and walks away.

Initials. Not mine, of course. Whose? Certainly Mark's and Adam's. What disloyalty if I didn't stand by them. It's not their fault that they're not here. And Sara would be furious to be left out. A good deed. I bend over, but Doug shows up and we go inside for my lesson.

Our class assignment is to contact a Holocaust survivor, and I write to the mother of one of Julia's classmates. The woman is my age, which would be Anne Frank's age today. Her sister was in the camp too. Both are now in New York. The idea is to ask one simple question, and I ask for her reaction to Steven Spielberg's epic *Schindler's List.* Her answer is matter-of-fact. Yes, a good film, that's the way it was. She and her husband and sister saw it. He is an American who had no experience of the war, and his wife's ordeal has not been a matter of deep or frequent discussion between them. He sat at the film between the two women, his head between his knees most of the time. The women spoke to each other quietly during the film, often over the bowed back of the wretched and retching husband: "Yes, that's right, oh yes, do you remember that?"

Norman Hanenbaum, from our band, brings his "challenged" choir to services. The choir includes a blind girl who sings powerfully and well. She is Catholic and spent a year in Israel and learned Hebrew and Yiddish songs. Two men, twins, look exactly like Tenniel's illustration of Tweedledee and Tweedledum. Norman's introduction is touching: he simply announces their names and tells us in what halfway house they're living, and when he comes to a name and says, "She's living independently," everyone in the choir says "*Yeah!*" and pumps. The Tweedles live at home with their parents. After every number they give each other robust high-five slaps.

Adam's mother is at the service and draws me aside and says she hears he's disruptive. I say I think he's a fine boy and remind her of his unashamed affection toward her when she picked him up one day, and I echo Rabbi Doug that any disruption will be cured by terror. The problem is, she says, he's bored. But his music is coming along well. The exchange leaves me feeling awkward, an informer in the class.

That Sunday we have an entertainer in school. He is young, tall and handsome, and he plays performance/parlor games with the whole group. Kids and teachers join in the games. I prefer to sit and watch. He's a sort of *tummler* and wears red suspenders and a shirt with profiles of jazz musicians on it. His good posture and curly hair begin to upset me, and I sit on pins and needles because at any moment he may turn into a mime and start my least favorite performance style. Years ago I began to see the abundance of deaf mimes, performers imitating hearing people who are pretending that they can't speak. I hate the heaviness of mime, I love the movement of sign, a real language that can express past and future as any real language can. If my doctor phoned—the old joke—and told me that I had only an hour or two to live, first I'd leave messages on the answering machines of my busy family, then I'd have a smoke on one of my old pipes—I do miss them. Then I'd go out and shoot a mime.

The performer leads us in a number game where seven is expressed as BOO! Then there is progressive storytelling, then people become clay blobs and are shaped and modeled. The parents mold the kids, then vice versa.

Back in class we learn that the Angel of Death can't take you when you're learning Torah. Is that how we can hang the bell on the Angel of Death?

On Tuesday my tutorial goes well enough. Doug starts me on the introductory prayer to the haftorah. He sings it and it's beautiful. Again he's cheerily helpful. "See, David? The musical notes are written exactly the same way! They just mean something different." Doug's knack of blending the bad news and the good news reminds me of Balanchine, who would leave my studio and I'd be so excited to pursue a new design idea that I would forget, for days, that he'd rejected a month's work.

Doug records the new prayer for me, singing it onto a cassette. All of our prayers and passages are on tapes that he has made for each of us. It must have been harder to study without the tape recorder, not yet invented when I was a boy. Maybe it was a more thorough learning process. I tell him that I've copied my tapes in case I lose one. "Good. You wouldn't believe . . . I mean it's not that they lose the tapes I make for them. My last adventure was with one of the kids who said, 'Well, no, Rabbi, I didn't exactly lose it. I recorded over it.'" So Doug had to listen to some horrifying song—he says it was about Green Death or something—before he could rerecord. He says that I can sing better than the Green Death vocalist.

On Wednesday, the 29th of January, class goes well enough, all present. Rachel shows real concern because Rebecca Price, who tutors us in Hebrew, is going to Israel. Doug says that we may go for some study to his house. "I'm not going," says Adam. Doug then says, "I want you to write—" "No," says Adam. "Writing is a great skill, Adam," says Doug. "No it's not" (muffled, Adam is back under the bookcase). Sara goes after Doug again about his hairline, and Doug tells the story of Elisha and the bears, which is in Kings. It seems that Elisha was taunted by little children (youths, in my Christian Bible) for his baldness. Elisha cursed them in the name of the Lord, and two she bears (sex not mentioned in the other Bible) came forth out of the woods and tore forty and two children (youths). Of course the story backfires. My classmates seem to have no fear whatsoever of bears, Doug is in a no-win situation. Later he tells me that while most little kids want the story of "The Three Bears," his daughter wants this story of bald Elisha and the bears. I suggest to Doug that there might be a Rabbi Protection Program.

Sunday, February 2nd, my father's birthday. We are all present, and after just a bit of classwork we come to my home, where Julia and Jack and I have remodeled a barn. My classmates like the space. Everyone has brought a Jewish dish—noodles, matzoh-ball soup, etc. I make borscht, but no one except me and Debbie like it.

Leonora is there, enjoying my crowd, and the gang run my electric trains. I worked hard to get these trains and the pesky short-circuiting loops of track ready for this day. With the exception of a few I bought for Dan, these trains are antiques, toys built before I was born, and I have one windup that was made the year of my mother's birth. It's a challenge to keep them all going. After our meal we watch a video about a teacher who, as an experiment, introduced fascist behavior into his class, the point being that his students were inspired by the discipline, camaraderie, and achievement until they saw the injustices.

On February 5th the school gathering starts with Doug saying, "I'll hold those until after class," and I turn to see Ben handing him a rugged pair of handcuffs. We talk about Madeleine Albright, the new Secretary of State, whose parents gave up Judaism and became Catholics in the thirties in Germany. The family then went to England, and she was never told about the conversion. Is she Jewish? She went from that Catholicism to being a Protestant anyway. Why not go back to Judaism? asks a boy. Perhaps she prefers one of the other religions, suggests Mark.

In our February 12th service, we use a *yad,* a pointer, to follow the words on the Torah. This is not only because one does not touch the holy scroll, but because the writing is done using traditional media, such as charcoal bound by oil and resin, and is easily rubbed off. *Yad* means "hand" and there is indeed a tiny hand at its end, the first finger pointing. It gives a delicacy and precision to the process, a tiny dramatic transformation. Also, you can't fool around with the work on this vellum, made from the skin of a ritually slaughtered animal. If there's a mistake, however small, a scribe must correct it.

The sermon today is by Eric, in the class below ours, and he speaks of people who say things that they don't really mean. He corrects statements made to him, such as "Merry Christmas," and tells the well-wisher that he's Jewish. This even includes, he says, stuff like "Season's Greetings," because he's not fooled by what "Season" means. Doug comments that it takes courage to come forward that way when you're in the minority.

In my tutorial I show that I'm starting to read the Torah writing. Doug tells me a touching story about the strength of these rituals. Rachel's older brother, also from Guatemala and even darker skinned, broke down during his bar mitzvah last year and wept on the bema. He said that for the first time he felt that he really belonged. This adopted child was undergoing a Jewish rite and coming into the "family." The ritual, arbitrary for many, was a vivid passage for him.

When we come to the *V'ahavta* prayer ("Thou shall love thy God . . .") I mimic Jami and ask Doug why he's so obsessed with that prayer. He laughs and says he's noticed that I'm getting more and more like the kids. Yes, I say, I'll be lugged off by the ear to the principal's office one of these days.

Then Doug describes one of the scenes from the recent weekend in Boston, unlamented in memory. Some DJ brought three dancing girls onstage. They were not heavily dressed, and the eyes of the boys were jumping out of their sockets when suddenly one of the most quiet and shy of all the boys was up onstage with the girls, and they were falling all over him, as we say. How did you do that? Doug later asked the boy. Well, they were working so hard, and I asked them if they'd like a glass of water. Our first Jewish president, says Doug.

Next week we are at the end of spring vacation, and attendance is poor. Rachel, Mark, Aaron, Alex and myself. Alex is emerging from soccer, and he is with us more, striving for the "Outrageous" medal, but only by fighting gravity and Debbie's conception of how one might sit properly on a chair. He just won't do it. Later, Doug joins us and says, "Feet down." "My feet are down," says Alex, meaning that they're hanging down. They're not touching the floor because the chair is tipped back. The deft and narrow definition tickles the class. It drives me toward crazy to see Doug not fly off the handle about this. I think of sawing the chair legs halfway through so that a tip angle of more than forty degrees will land the boys clattering on the floor. Then I read my Anne Frank essay to them. It seems to be well received. Doug makes no comment, but Mark stands up and applauds wildly. "You should get it published in *The New Yorker*," he says. Lary phones me the next day and says he heard that Anne Frank was "tremendous."

After class I ask Doug about the tipped-chair scene. "If your work is to teach Hebrew, you've got to have endless patience," he says. I say that I understand a personality that may have boundless patience, but my question, really, is about open insubordination and how you handle it. He says, "I know that in the end I will win. Always." He tells me that there are so many things I don't see—his chats with the kids at their homes and with their parents, and the resultant discipline. "Is it your perception, Doug, that the other kids see this boy's acts, reprimanded frequently during that class by you and modified only slightly by him and not corrected—do the other kids see this as his triumph of insubordination, or yours of patience?" Doug struggles with this question and does not have a ready answer. "I can tell you that the few times that I've lost my temper have all turned out badly." Why does Doug put up with this? I'm catching on. It's simply like my old theater work. No matter how miserable the process, we would eventually have an opening night, and probably a party. The work at hand would be over. Doug knows that he's not teaching Latin, where the benefits might not occur to the student for years. He's headed toward a culminating event that will prove its worth there and then, at least for the time being.

Wednesday, February 26th. "Today," says Doug, "will be our most—" "Boring day," says Adam. Doug says, "Right, most boring day. It's time to get your *tuchises,* your *tuchi,* in gear." So we study the prayer before the reading of the haftorah. I team up with Hannah, and she helps me learn it. She knows it already. While choosing up these pairs, I hear Jami say, "No, not him!" but I don't know who she doesn't want. It seems that the feeling is mutual. The teams are adjusted.

Then Doug tells the story of the old Jewish man, whose name has been lost, who was being forced to slaughter a pig in submission to the God-Emperor Antiochus. This is the beginning of the great Maccabee story. The knife was tremblingly raised when suddenly a priest darted forward and killed the old man. We'd celebrate the priest today if he'd killed *himself* in protest, I'm about to say, but Mark is quicker and leaps to his feet. "A horrible story," he shouts. "Pigs have feelings too, you know!" Doug speaks about our sermons and says that they should relate to the Torah text read that day. Jami: "Are you serious, Rabbi?"

Later I learn, to my dismay, the definition of kosher wine. I had asked this, wondering if only grapes with cloven hooves were smashed in the bathtubs, and Doug put me off, perhaps because there were people in the room he didn't want to offend. Now he tells me, sheepishly, that it means wine that has not been touched by a gentile. "What?" I exclaim. "I believe," he explains, "that in ancient times some wines were part of the festivities of others, Bacchants for example, that offended the Jews." It's a miserable definition, he agrees. Also you can boil it, he says, which may not improve the taste. Some Jews may not want an unknown waiter to handle the bottle, preferring to uncork it with their own hands.

We learn that the dietary laws, keeping kosher, are confusing to some degree and misunderstood to a larger degree, and I will here add to the confusion. I've not been raised in a kosher house and don't follow the rules. Julia, at thirteen, wanted to follow the rules because she admired a classmate who did: it seemed a special and distinctive and disciplined lifestyle, and that may be the best reason of all to keep kosher. She kept at it for a month or two, until lobster season. Rules that make distinctions are often good: wasn't it special, if you are Catholic, to have sat at McDonald's at 11:59 P.M. Friday night, poised over a Big Mac, waiting for midnight? Where has that gone?

The word *kosher* basically means "fitting" or "proper." The word *kadosh* (holy), has as its original meaning "separateness," or "separation," and Leviticus is a book of separation, of right from wrong. The basic kosher rules are set forth in Leviticus 11. Eat meat if the animal, domestic only, has a cloven hoof and chews its cud. A camel chews cud but does not have the cloven hoof. Pigs have the cloven hooves but don't chew cud. Rabbits chew cud but have the wrong feet. Some of this may be based on inexact science: rabbits appear to chew cud but they don't, they just munch. Camels really do have a cloven hoof. Pawed animals are not kosher because that's like walking on your hands, which is unacceptable. Also no crawling kinds of things, ranging from snakes to weasels.

Leonora was taught that these are commonsense health rules, but there's more to it than that. One may eat fish with scales, but nothing from the water that does not have scales. Birds and animals that are predators and tear flesh are *trayf.* Don't eat eagles, owls, and so forth, nor bats, which must have seemed birdlike. Chickens and ducks are vegetarians and fine, so are their eggs *if not fertilized.* No seagulls—there even I would draw the line. Owl would be okay for me if it were raised for eating and not spotted and taken from the wild. Today environmental attitudes often take center stage. I know a vegetarian who defines his habit simply: "I eat nothing with a central nervous system."

Certain insects are okay, if a locust sandwich seems tempting, and most insects are plentiful today. You can't eat bees but you can eat their honey—perhaps the one case where you are permitted to eat the product of a forbidden creature.

There could be other factors involved here. For example, re-calling the logic of the wine, pigs were used by some cults in devil worship. Don't eat what your enemy worships. And of course common sense does apply, and Doug's theory makes sense to me: if Schlomo said he wanted to eat cow that night, and Yankle said he was tired of cow and wanted Bengal tiger, we are more likely to have Schlomo as an ancestor.

When—and where—I grew up, Chinese food was more popu-lar than today, because Japanese or Indian or Vietnamese or Thai restaurants were not yet in active competition. Many of those in my boyhood community who kept kosher exempted Chinese food—it seemed a diet unto itself, and a little pork in an egg roll didn't count. It's hard to imagine that we count 5758 years old as I write this, and China claims only 4500 or so years, therefore Jews had to suffer for over a thousand years without Chinese food! To-day one sees more signs for kosher Chinese food.

There are also rules for preparation, and if the carcass of an unclean animal, say a snake, falls into an earthen vessel, you can't drink the water it contains and you must break the vessel. If an unclean carcass falls on a seed that is to be sown, that's okay, but if the seed is wet, it becomes unclean. Even if it's an acceptable animal, such as a cow, unclean could mean that it died of natural causes or was incorrectly slaughtered. Ritual slaughter, including how to avoid eating blood and much else, is complex. And we are told in our texts, in no uncertain terms, that these regulations do not require explanation. Just do it, for discipline and moral conduct and simply because God said to do it. Or, a good reason to many, to imbue the primitive animal function of eating with an element of sacredness.

Note *earthen* vessel. Clay, porous. If it were stone, the same rule might not apply. Today glass plates are used by some to avoid having separate plates for dairy dishes and meat dishes. That separation, going as far as having separate kitchens in kosher restaurants, comes from Moses' declaration, mentioned three times in the Torah, that one must not seethe a kid in its mother's milk. My friend Willy Nolan was raised in a Jewish neighborhood in New York City, and he would laugh and say that he still couldn't eat butter with his pork.

If Bernstein asks how much is that bacon, and a clap of thunder rocks the supermarket, he can rightfully look up and say, "Thanks for the warning, but I was only asking!" Is he right? I'm sure that there's been plenty of rabbinical discussion, and this kind of joke could develop into a discussion in our study. As you know, if you shoot a man who is already dead, you can't be accused of murder. But if you thought he was alive, can you be accused of attempted murder?

Leonora says, "David will eat anything. He gouges himself."

We talk also about the Sabbath. Only one thing can excuse

breaking, or desecrating the Sabbath, and that is saving a human life. To many, this holy day, set aside, is the cornerstone of our beliefs. My friend Paul Shulman told the story of a ship he was commanding that was jammed with refugees heading for Israel. They stopped for fuel, and the Sabbath evening fell. When they started up again, Orthodox Jews raced to the bridge and said he couldn't start the engines. "But they've never stopped," said Paul, who feared to pause any longer, in perilous waters, with his ship full of passengers. Okay, they said, but you can't start motion again after stopping the ship. "No," cried Paul, "we've never stopped! We've been continuously moving forward and backward, slowly, at the dock!"

On the next Saturday we eat a Sabbath lunch, all of us, the parents at one end of our long skinny table, me and Doug and the other students at the other end. I'm reprimanded because I don't eat my vegetables. I'm the only who must be excused to drive to baby-sit my grandchildren.

The 12th of March, an awful day. A dear and dedicated congregant, Joe Friend, dies, literally in front of Doug, who is setting up to speak at a senior center in a nearby town. Then Doug drives to Hartford Hospital to tell this to the new widow, Lillian, who is recovering from bypass surgery. This is a Wednesday. Donna Moran, yes, a convert, who has headed our Religious Affairs Committee, leads our class. Kids love torturing a substitute teacher. We struggle through a word-by-word translation of the *Avot* prayer. Then Debbie leads the service, and we all speak in turn, and the afternoon is basically productive. I meet Doug Friday morning and say in answer to his question that, no, no one was killed in class during his absence and that if he wanted a more cheerful answer, he'd have to ask someone else.

My daughter, Julia, phones. She has gotten my progress report from Hebrew school, and I'm doing well. I had it sent to her rather than my wife. You understand. From Debbie: "Effort and Enthusiasm: 1. Class Participation: 1. Homework Preparation: 1. Comes Prepared with books, pencils, paper, etc.: 1." (1 is the top mark, Excellent; 2 is Very Good; 3, Good; 4, Needs Improvement. What happened to "Unsatisfactory?")

> Although David professes to have difficulty learning to read a new language at his age, he has made excellent progress in Hebrew this year. He has learned not only a new alphabet, but is able to decode unfamiliar words with ease. David is becoming familiar with all the prayers in the morning service in preparation for his bar mitzvah, and is able to read competently the Shema, *Barechu,* Torah blessings, and *V'ahavta.* I have no doubt that David will soon master all of the required prayers. . . . In our bar/bat mitzvah curriculum, David has grasped the issues and understands the material we have covered. He struggles with many of his beliefs, yet clearly articulates his doubts, questions, and opinions on aging, religion, and God. David's work in all content areas is carefully prepared and well developed. At first, David had trouble completing assignments in a timely manner, but he is learning to write more freely. David's book report on *The Diary of Anne Frank* was well written, creative and provocative. I hope that he will continue to work on this story and submit it for publication. David is an asset to Kitah

Vav and it is a treat having him in class. I hope he will
continue in his search for an understanding of his beliefs and in his study of Hebrew and Judaism.

Rabbi Doug emphasizes that I have a "particular aptitude in
grasping theological/spiritual concepts." He gives me an unusually
high mark, 1+, for coming prepared with books, pencils, paper.

My mother kept our report cards, all of them, from kindergarten on. She said this with relish to Anwar Sadat's widow at a
graduation ceremony at Wesleyan University, where I received an
honorary degree. My brother and I could see the report cards any
time we wanted to, she said, which meant never. I found mine in a
shoe box when we moved her from her Stamford apartment at age
ninety. Julia points out that if she had known that I was to get another report card, she would have stayed alive.

Tuesday morning I go to the funeral of Sid Slater, a loving
woman who battled cancer for twenty years and managed careers
during the battle, working with us at the theater all too briefly.
Doug officiates, and as always what he touches becomes filled with
grace. This is in West Hartford, in the Jewish mortuary that is *the*
place to be. The room is a mishmash, but the feeble attempt at design is distinctly Egyptian. I wonder at our efforts to escape from
Egypt, and now we die and go back there?

On the next day Doug tells me of his frequent conversations
with the owner of the mortuary. "Why do you use all those *other*
places? Why let your people use those *other* services? Who is this
Swan Funeral Home? Swan? So what kind of a name is that?"

Chapter 18

✡ ✡ ✡

My Essay on Anne Frank

The fact is that I've taken advantage of the class to continue work on a piece. It was my idea, not to claim that it's new under the sun: what if Anne Frank were alive today? I thought of it as a play, but gave it to my friend, the brilliant author Joanne Greenberg, hoping for a story from which a play could be made. And so she wrote it, and the attitude of Anne Frank and most ideas that are good come from Joanne. But then she wanted to stop, and I asked if I could continue it and rewrite it for my class, and she said sure, why not. Her version was longer. I may have condensed it too much and made it too much of a monologue, just the bare bones for a dramatist to flesh out. Here it is as I read it in class.

• • •

What if, try to imagine, Anne Frank suddenly appeared alive among us? It could happen. A dozen scenarios could explain how she survived the camp, and there could be as many reasons why she waited until now to reveal herself.

Perhaps she is in this country, it doesn't matter exactly where, perhaps closing a house for her best friend, who had emigrated to this country and then died from a long illness. This story could be taking place in one of these little towns, Chester or Deep River. Perhaps Anne was returning to her home in Europe and was in an accident, perhaps a car struck her, perhaps then her money and her passport were stolen. The passport was not in her own name but in the name of a young woman who died, and then Anne took her name, in the camp at Bergen. Perhaps the dead girl was the daughter of a Kapo, a Jew who squealed on her fellow prisoners and was given protection in exchange. Anne, whom she liked, could now be smuggled real food and medicines under the name of the dead daughter. Perhaps only two days before our story begins this woman, who says she was born Anne Frank, uttered that famous name, unused by her for over fifty years. Perhaps she was disoriented in the hospital. Stranger things happen every day. What interests us most is what she would say.

She's not so very old, just sixty-eight as I write this, a year minus ten days older than me. A Gemini. Would I have remembered a girl a year ahead of me if I had been in the Lyceum for Jewish Students in Amsterdam? We would have been shifted to this school when the Germans came in. A shy dark-haired girl, pleased that boys liked her. Would I even have known that she was Jewish until they put the yellow armbands on us and herded us into these cramped rooms? We didn't make much of our religion until then. Perhaps I knew that her father had fought for Germany in the Great War and that they had moved here, wealthy upper-class and assimilated people, once a part of the great financial community of

Frankfurt. Now, well-heeled in Amsterdam, was it vanity that made them believe that they would always be accepted here? Ah, the mistake, discovered too late. That mistake killed them all except, ironically, Otto Frank, the family leader. Or so we all believe.

Now I see this woman sitting in a room, a rabbi's study, not large, with books on every wall and piled on every table and on the floor. In the room with the rabbi are a psychiatrist, who is a friend of the rabbi, and another man, the president of the synagogue. Perhaps they are joined by a nun, or novice, who sat with the woman in the hospital. Perhaps Anne, and I shall call her by that name, wears a cast on a broken wrist. Perhaps these people want to help her, but only the nun accepts her as the real Anne Frank.

The psychiatrist, Hirsch, has evaluated her and determined in his report that she is sane. But his curiosity has continued, and his job is not finished to his satisfaction. Many people are deluded about their identities, but in this case he is sure that it is not a psychosis. Anyway, an Anne Frank sighting is more interesting to him than an Elvis sighting, and perhaps there's a scholarly paper in it. He has assembled friends to hear her story because she needs money to continue her trip. Bloom, the rabbi, wants to help her, whoever she is. The president of the synagogue, Silverman, believes that this obvious impostor will make him and the congregation a laughingstock. Finally Sister Emily, who assists the psychiatrist in the hospital, believes in miracles. It is a miracle to her that she is in the same room with the diarist who illuminated her Christian faith and who gave her the inspiration and strength to work and study for her vows.

Look at Anne. How do you see her? Can you see her? Is she frozen in time forever, frozen for you on the cover of the paperback, in a picture taken when she was perhaps eleven, younger than you, my classmates, and four years before she supposedly died? I see her, cruelly perhaps, as my own age, or is this length of life a cruelty? I see a woman of medium height, muscular, with graceful, long-fingered but strong hands. She wears a dark denim skirt and a cotton blouse, and she has tied a small kerchief loosely around her neck. She is wearing the sport sneakers that so many of us wear today, without stockings, and we can see blue gatherings of veins on strong legs. Her hair is short, a silver wash-and-wear hairdo. She is no longer doe eyed, not innocent as you've seen her; her eyes are dark and piercing, and under them are deep shadows and pouches. Her mouth does not rest in a smile. Yes, there is an aristocratic look to her, particularly in the alert way she holds her head. But her movements are not delicate; they are sharp and purposeful. She turns quickly, even abruptly, to people who speak to her, but in her answers she may turn her head away and soften the directness of her words. She will often stare at the books on the wall, she will leave long pauses between her phrases, and then she will turn back and focus, a sudden, surprising move. She would be speaking American English in the clipped and harsh accents of Israelis, emphasizing the final consonants that Americans slide over. She would have learned basic English in school. She would also know German and some Yiddish. Her Dutch would be old-fashioned and formal, and now she pronounces the name as "Anna Fronk." The conversation has been going on.

"Do you hear voices?" asks Hirsch, the psychiatrist.

"Sometimes I do now," she says, "but not at first, most of us succeeded in putting the voices behind us, and after two years in the displaced persons shelter, I thought I had said good-bye to every smell or sound or taste that reminded me of the murderers and the murdered. Then I went to Israel, to new languages, Hebrew and more English, to new streets, to new air and water, to new stones. But for years I didn't look into the night sky because I feared I would see familiar stars."

"The voices?" asks Hirsch.

"Later, later, the memories came, in waves, catching moments only, because it's too big, too vast, but despite all you do to protect yourself, your senses betray you—you hear a bucket tipped over in the dark, you smell wet straw, you see blood spattered from a slaughtered animal, washing away in rain. This came with the Eichmann trial. I didn't even know who he was, but there were films, that first wave carrying back the memories, the faces in camp, even the voices came back to us, they were in our heads and they came back. After the trial you would see people stopping and just standing in the streets, crying without covering their faces or quieting their voices."

"Dreams?" asks Hirsch.

"Yes, just moments, quick snapshots, but in the mornings I woke as a wife, a mother, a farmworker, a teacher. I could throw this back at the memories of nakedness, of stiffened corpses, I drowned them in the sweat of work, in the tears of family life, in the water I carried for our orchards on the kibbutz. I was too busy, I was too tired."

"And why didn't you change back to your identity after the war?" asks Silverman, the president of the synagogue.

"I was afraid of the bureaucrats, they were so precise. My new papers were in order, I had no old papers. Then I was married and pregnant under my new identity, learning to be a border guard, learning how to fire a rifle."

Sister Emily winces. "A gun? You shot a gun?"

"Yes, an M-1, left from the war, we didn't have our Uzis yet. The rifle was heavy for me. I never shot anyone, but I was ready to kill for my children and my husband, even for our gardens. Is that impossible for you to imagine, Sister? Anne Frank armed? Anne Frank stealing someone's food in the camp to stay alive? Can you imagine her stealing a dead girl's shoes?"

Bloom asks, "And your fame? Your diaries? You must have known of them."

"Yes, Rabbi, I heard of them and I read them, but that was years later. Then I knew of the play, the movie, even the lawsuits about copyright. Should I have stepped forward and lose the life I had worked so hard to create? Lose my husband, my young family, the farming that I loved? Should I spend the rest of my life reliving what I wanted to forget? Rabbi, I barely remembered the diary, the camp blew out the candle on that past, Amsterdam was cold and scattered ashes to me. I felt no claim to the diary. These were only my private thoughts. I was now a stranger to that young girl from some other and older world. Yes, it was good writing, perceptive and touching. It was like the crayon pictures full of wonder that my own young children drew, and then they lost that wonder that young children have when they are seeing what they believe. We grow up and then we believe what we see, and it's never as much or as clear."

In the tones of a prosecutor, Silverman asks, "And why now? If hiding has been so important to you, why do you reveal yourself now?"

Anne pauses. "I do not fully understand that myself. I was distraught from my friend's death. I knew that my money and my precious passport, my identity, were gone. My jewelry, things of no real value except to me, things that my husband gave me, that was gone. Maybe it was the concussion. I spoke out of the past. And now I will stay Anne Frank. My children have careers, I have grandchildren, my husband is dead, he was killed in a border raid. My father is dead."

Hirsch speaks. "Tell us about your father. Did you ever see him after the war?"

"In a dream only, in a vivid dream, a dream I resisted because it was so real that I didn't want to see him crumble in flames or fall and be carted away in a wheelbarrow with other stiff corpses. I knew he had a new life, a new marriage. He recognized me after I told him small indisputable things, a lipstick color, something that my sister got for her birthday. I was in camp with my mother when she died, and my sister, he knew that. Finally, in the dream, he accepted as his daughter this farm woman with a rifle slung over her shoulder. He was horrified to see me as I was, to see destroyed all the years of European polish, refinement that generations of wealthy Jews had acquired. This loss of gentility seemed to mean more to him than that I had survived."

"Did he say anything?"

"It was all in his face, but I remember words, a few, spoken or not spoken. He begged me to stay hidden because that way I was of more value to my people. I believed that, then, and in my dream I had a father's affirmation. It became strange, I saw his face but it was burned out, like the gutted buildings with empty window frames."

There is a pause. Anne goes to the coffeemaker and draws a cup. She holds the mug in her full hand, two fingers going through the handle, army style. Black coffee. "But, in a dream?" asks Sister Emily. "I would have gone to him, after that, and really spoken to him."

"You? You of all people? You don't believe in the dreams? I understood it not as a visit from a heavenly messenger, but because it made my own thoughts clear. No, let it be, I said to myself. I didn't want to visit him and repeat the dream, and hear again that I was better hidden, better dead, and perhaps hear that his living was the royalties on the memory of me. This is not easy to say. Lucky for him that I didn't return to the annex before him, after the war, find the diaries, and probably lose them, as one does."

"Lucky for all of us," says Sister Emily.

"So you believe. You told me yourself how many others besides Jews have modeled their lives on Anne Frank. How many like you, devoted to Christian faith, read what was endured and were affirmed by a girl who could say, 'I still believe that people are really good at heart.' Yes, like my children's crayon drawings. But no one wants to remember the last line of the diary, the very last, that I wrote a few days before the Germans broke in and carted us away. Do you remember it, my friends? It was about what I could be, what I aspired to be if, 'if there weren't any other people living in the world.'

"Endured, affirmation. What had I endured? A comfortable hiding place lined with my father's money? Nothing, nothing was endured until after the diary was left behind and forgotten, nothing was endured before the camp. That famous statement of a schoolgirl's faith works only when it's a monument to a dead girl. If I'd survived as Anne Frank, would the diaries have even been printed? And if they had been, what? One or two literary critics waiting for my first novel? My death was needed to glorify, to endorse, to proclaim the diary, to tattoo Belsen on all of us."

I can see the end of the string of numbers on her arm, it shows just above the cast, on an inch of puffed-out flesh below her rolled-up sleeve. The seven is notched in the European way, now blurred and faded, but a testament to German precision. Anne lights a small cigar, the cheap kind with a plastic holder. She draws in the smoke, it curls out of her nostrils. Silverman can't hide a smile.

She catches his expression. "Yes, your Anne Frank smoking a cigar. They were a comfort on cold nights at the border when the wind wouldn't betray me. If I had lived on in Amsterdam, with no war, you'd be seeing me in a fashionable restaurant smoking with a long ivory holder, like Roosevelt? And I'm not one of your saints, Sister. Saints have to be willing to die, don't they? I wasn't willing to die."

"As your father said in the dream, wouldn't the real Anne Frank want to stay dead to help her people?" asks Silverman.

"That fourteen-year-old girl, the one who is real to you, she is long gone. I'm the real Anne Frank, today's Anne Frank, a woman born from that girl in horrible labor before I was sixteen. And no, I don't want to stay dead, I don't want any longer to give in as Jesus did to the fourth temptation in the desert, give in to Satan's clever temptation to die on the cross to serve his people." She laughs for the first time, a deep laugh, an unexpected and jarring laugh from the girl on the cover of the paperback. "I read those sentences in a novel. Blasphemy, Sister?" Or the preacher's remark, "Get off the cross, we need the wood."

Bloom picks up. "Please, you tell us what that means."

"I believe that the preacher meant that the message of the crucifixion was the resurrection, the new life, not the death on the cross but the rebirth from death, the liberation, the same as Passover. But I'm not religious. I wasn't even the best person hiding in that annex. At that age, you know, twelve, I was a nudnik, a stiff pain in the *tuchis*. Everyone was more patient, everyone but me had moments of greatness, but I'm remembered because of a schoolgirl's diary. This weighs on me like a tombstone. I'm trying to crawl out from under my own tombstone. The preacher may have meant, simply, let's get on with it, on with it, now. Make some use of these beliefs, don't sit and wallow in them. I saw the movie about us. We weren't a religious family. We were too modern, too secular, but we kept some of the old rituals, maybe from habit. In the movie they played these rituals as something general, laundered we say, no Hebrew, something vaguely holy, something to show that we suffered because of some sweet holiness, not because of our ancient Jewishness with an out-of-date language and behavior that could be off-putting to Episcopalians, so get off the Jewishness, we need the box office."

"And now," says Bloom, "do you believe?"

Anne draws warm coffee and lifts her mug. "L'Chaim, Rabbi. That's an Israeli toast, Sister, it's Hebrew. It means 'To Life!' I'll tell you, Bloom, what I believe. L'Chaim is what I believe."

"I know some Hebrew, I've studied it, many of us do," says Sister Emily.

"It won't help us here," says Anne. "I'll speak English, but Yiddish is the language to use when you're annoyed."

"It's a dying language," says Silverman.

"Don't bet on that. Sure it's dying, dying with your kind of Jew, who has only some warped pride, yes, pride in the Holocaust that singles us out, you hang on to that because it's the best way you know to give us pride as a people. Otherwise you want to be mixed in, homogenized, you know. I have a different Jew in mind. Your kind will die out as Jews, not mine. But we weren't the only people that died, Silverman. I saw others, deaf people, politicals, homosexuals, other people who died only because they couldn't speak German. I saw them one day, standing in line in a freezing rain, naked men and women and children, waiting almost two hours in line because the gas chamber was broken, waiting until it was fixed. They weren't sheep, Silverman, not meek, but by then we all knew that every tiny resistance, even falling out of line, killed twenty extra."

Silverman stands. "Whoever you are, you're smart and I like you. I believe, at the least, that you were in the camps, and my heart goes out to you. Rabbi, I have a trustee's meeting at Birchwood and I'm fishing for a big gift. Wish me luck. Ma'am, Dr. Hirsch, Sister, excuse me."

Bloom picks up again. "I give a lecture on Talmud, five show up. I talk about the Holocaust, a hundred show up. Our interfaith activities are based on Holocaust anniversaries, on Anne Frank's birthday. Our fund-raising depends on Anne Frank, on the Holocaust."

"Thank you, Rabbi. Well, here I am, uncomfortably alive. I don't want to spoil your interfaith rallies and I know you need money. I need money now, I want to get to Amsterdam."

Hirsch speaks. "Amsterdam? I thought . . ."

"Yes, Amsterdam. You know who the hero is? Not me, I wrote a diary. The real hero is Miep. I want to see her grave. That's what I'm most ashamed of; I've never gone back, I've never seen her since the war. I've been afraid to return to a place that I cannot control. Do you believe that here, in this town, there is anyone who would give shelter to a family and feed them for two years if discovery meant their own deaths? Eh, Rabbi?"

Anne looks at the books lining the walls. "And this is your hiding place, your book fortress, Rabbi? I saw them burned. Books burn quickly and easily. We would have burned them in the camp to keep us warm, do you think so? Incidentally, I don't see those volumes they sell that give you instant ready-made sermons."

Now Bloom laughs. "I write my sermons myself. It's hard and it takes a lot of time. I'm tempted to buy that set."

"I sympathize. A new thought every week. Yes, it takes a lot of energy and time. Time taken from what? From your religious studies and your teaching? Or from the weeks of time spent on the sermons and the gatherings you run on the Holocaust? Are the gatherings for your president, Silverman? For his idea of how to keep a congregation stuck together for his fund-raising? For a new synagogue? A better living for you, and you deserve it? Rabbi, we sit in your room surrounded by religious books, even holy books. The Holocaust is not religion, it is not belief, Rabbi! The Holocaust was a political event. Are you a political scientist, Rabbi, or a holy man? The old Anne Frank did not die for her beliefs, she died because of them. But they were unexamined beliefs. You understand that, Sister? If she had been given the chance, would she have changed her religion? A young, pretty girl, just becoming a woman, with her life ahead? A martyr wouldn't have changed beliefs. Silverman would have, he thinks beliefs are community activities. Don't preach beliefs to him, Rabbi, he'll think he's gone to the wrong meeting. I doubt if he's ever thought ten minutes about God. Nor, Rabbi, had I."

Hirsch is stirred. Old family memories. He isn't a believer, he loves and is married to a gentile woman whose family wouldn't attend the wedding. "Tell me more, anything, about your beliefs, in the camp, after the camp. You said you were not a believer when you were hidden in the annex. Have you, since—I mean do you now, did you?"

"In the camp? I was a young girl, I saw men and women praying, I saw shaking old men pulling rags over their shoulders to pray, crying to heaven. The guards laughed and just shot them. They had no time to deal with the old ones who would shriek to God as they were dragged away in the mud. And I had no time to ponder beliefs. I schemed to steal food.

"Rabbi, do you remember how much I wrote about a girl becoming a woman, in our hiding place? You know. That stopped when I was sick, when I was starving. It stopped for many of the full-grown women too, they told me. When we were put in a camp by the Allies and fed and given clothes and beds, it started again. It started again for me in the late spring of 1945, when the world changed color for us, from black and gray to green, and spring was there again. It started again for me when we were being walked on a path among trees. I wept, Rabbi, do you understand, Sister? I wept for the first time in a year, in that bright green, with my own blood flowing again. There were wildflowers. Maybe I was closer to God just then, closer than before or since in my life, in that time, what, fifteen minutes? But there was horror left in us, who could think? We still had nightmares. But on that day, in that bright green with a clear blue sky, God could have sent the rainbow again. He didn't, you know. I remember all of this only now, Hirsch, thank you. And then I met my husband in that camp, and then we were married and I had babies and then I flowed with milk, but that's when we ourselves are all gods and goddesses, isn't it?"

Anne lights up again, she is impatient now and walks around the room, stepping over the piles of books and magazines. "Maybe if I had gone to our God then I wouldn't have kept so hidden for so long. But what could I have accepted, then?"

Sister Emily says, in a tremulous voice, she is close to tears, "Anne, it's not important whether or not you believed, or whether you chose or not to die. We need our symbols, you know that, realities become our myths, our icons. God is so hard for all of us to conceive, Anne, you understand, and you understand that Jesus was a man, or a man in form, the son of God to many of us, and you understand that we can see him and talk to him, understand Jesus who walked on our streets with us. The way we think of you is not as a god or as a saint, but as just one life, a precious life that we saw through your eyes in your beautiful writing, and that one young life we can understand, because the rest is too vast for us, yes, your one cut-off life is our bridge to the camps and the horror."

Anne laughs again. "Beautiful, Sister, as beautiful as you are. Yes, the God who was on earth, even a man, so we can contact Him, that's the genius of Christianity, we don't have it yet, maybe never. My life, through my useful death, means a lot to others. I understand. But I didn't sacrifice, as you would like to believe, no, I was simply murdered. Your yearning for my noble sacrifice has served its purpose, a bad purpose. Ach, look ahead! Sister, you've built your values on a great prophet's life and you can govern your life by those beliefs and values, and if Jesus' death was political, you made faith from it and proceeded from there. We are held back, we did the opposite, we substituted the politics for the faith. For the genuine faith of so many who were slaughtered, we have a substitution, the idea that we have something going for us because of their deaths. But have we no better system to unite us, to glorify us, than what someone else did to us? And when is our resurrection, Sister?"

Bloom speaks gently, "I have so much difficulty with my students, who can't understand a God that could have let that happen to us."

"Rabbi, life is quieter for me now and I search now for God as hard as Silverman searches for money. Money to support what, that same search for God among your congregants? No, more likely a better yield on your endowment, eh? I may have an answer to my search by the time I die, if I live a little longer, God willing. Meanwhile, I follow His law, I behave myself to other people.

"I read a Russian novel, and I remember, 'Believe but what your heart does say / No signs from heaven come today.' Tell your students, Rabbi, that you had a conversation with Anne Frank and she believes that God does not hold our hands anymore. She believes that God is not responsible for Auschwitz. Sister, do you know what that's from? 'No signs from heaven come today?' In the novel, Jesus appears among you, centuries ago, in Spain. There is an inquisition and the wise men question Him and condemn Him to death. They don't want Him alive, He's done His work, it's all been edited now, arranged the way they can use it, so don't make waves. Oh, they let Him go, because He promises to keep his mouth shut. I'm no Jesus, but I know that all of you wish I had stayed dead, I know you don't want this worn-down woman, who carried a rifle on the perimeter of an orange grove, Anne Frank with varicose veins, the imperfect mother just as you were imperfect parents, Anne Frank, the girl led away from her hiding place who didn't even scream out her life in the gas chamber but died a gentle death for you, the poster girl for the Holocaust, and so now young students can be touched without crossing that threshold to hell itself, to horror that I still cannot conceive. And aren't you glad that because of me and that silly sentence that I reject now, reject, aren't you glad that you can, through those few words, even find a way to forgive? And aren't you all so very fortunate that I was pretty, and not an ugly child?"

· · ·

That's as far as my imagination carries me, but I can wonder if this woman, Anne Frank or not, got her money, went to Amsterdam to visit Miep's grave, and then went home to Israel. I wonder if Hirsch pondered his faith after listening to her? Did he write his paper? I wonder if Rabbi Bloom ever talked to Silverman about the needs of the congregation?

Who might have found the money for Anne's trip home? Sister Emily? Why not? We can imagine the nun going to a man who had promised a favor, money if she needed it, a man whose dying mother she had comforted. But what if he is a biker in his ammunition shop who preaches that there had never been a Holocaust, a man who ignites hatred toward Jews and their "conspiracy"? But a promise is a promise, and he gives the money to Sister Emily. Does Anne care? I see her laughing again, saying to the biker: "Well, we're both tattooed, and you'd better help all the Jews you can, because you'll need us to hate. Maybe you'll keep alive the story of the Holocaust, and I need that to fight." I can see Emily weeping with mortification in the cab to the airport, saying, "I had no idea he was like that." "Tush," says Anne, "if only saints could bring us hot suppers we'd all starve." I see them parting in front of the baggage X-ray, and Sister Emily asking her what she intends to do when she gets home, and Anne might say, "I'm not sure. Maybe I'll try to write."

Chapter 19

✻ ✻ ✻

MY CLOSE BRUSH WITH
THE NOBEL PRIZE

I GO TO THE MEMORIAL SERVICE of my beloved college professor and tutor John Coolidge. His wife is blind now and
doesn't come to the reception afterward, but their daughter
and I share a brief moment. Yes, she remembers me. I saw her last
when she was about twelve, my own alter age now. She was a sweet
pretty child, shy and polite, and now she is a grandmother and is
handsome in that Cambridge lady style, tweedy, erect and alert.
The service is in the graceful Memorial Church and is well attended and awful. The academics who speak all say the same thing,
stylishly from time to time. To paraphrase: "This was a brilliant,
brilliant man, witty, so knowledgeable, so kind, so perceptive, a
paragon. We often sat together and talked about *everything* half the
night." Narcissists, their pools will cloud. This can get worse, and I
was present when certain alumni awards were being presented at
nearby Boston University. A short and stout professor was receiv-

ing his due, and he chose to thank and honor his own father. "He was also a great man," he said.

Golda Meier said, "Don't be humble, you're not so great."

Leonora says, "He likes to picture himself as an ignonymous person."

Memorial Church is restful and a good place to worship. That, to me, means to sit quietly and recall the people I care for, my own little memorial to the loveliness and lunacies of those who are physically gone. When I recall them they are still present in a sense, and it's as simple as that. And so after the service I sit for a few moments, as I've sat in this calming way in churches and cathedrals all over the world. Synagogues are usually locked, for sad reasons. Churches such as this remind me of pilgrims who left their country to establish their own bigotry in a new world. "For religious freedom," our children are taught. The thought can make anyone laugh. So be it, at least this architect was skilled: he copied another architect's work and left us this serene building.

I think of my friends who are dead, and there are plenty of them. I began work in New York as a young man, and for some years I was billed as "Broadway's Youngest Designer," but this was temporary billing at best, ticking away, waiting for the inevitable announcement from the maternity ward. I was linked with directors many years senior to me, and they died or retired. Sir Tyrone Guthrie, Elia Kazan, George Balanchine. As an apprentice I worked in London for men with names you might have known, dead now. You can date me as an apprentice (do we still know that word?) because I did the working drawings for *The Mousetrap*, still running as I write this forty-five years later. Then I worked in New York, and the great men who built and painted my sets died—Willy Nolan—or retired, Peter Feller. My teachers who cared for me are dead: Jo Mielziner, Don Oenslager, Roger Furse, Leslie Hurry, Ray Sovey; or retired, Bob O'Hearn. I have a compulsion to mention these names, and I've listed more elsewhere. You may not remember them, but I say them to myself, and once in a while, when I have a chance to speak publicly, I mention a name or two because I want the air to hear these names again. Someone I love said to me that she was moved by that, and so I continue to bore others with the habit. Maybe just thinking their names, or saying them out loud, is my contribution to the world. This is, Rabbi Doug tells me, an important tradition in our faith. Remember the names, honor them by remembering. We must not forget, we must not blot them out.

Joe Dalet, and that may not even be the correct spelling of his name, went from my little private high school into the Abraham Lincoln Brigade in the late thirties, and he was killed in Spain fighting the fascist Franco, Hitler's ally. When the Second World War ended in 1945, we planted trees to honor our graduates who had died, but the school refused to have one planted for Joe. It wasn't for the reason stated—that the death was in another country's civil war and before Pearl Harbor. It was because of the Communist taint of the brigade. Years later I was the speaker at the graduation ceremony of this high school, and after the usual inspirational comments (talk about speaking to thin air!) I added that footnote about Joe and said that I had brought a tree, and that although I never knew Joe, I was going to plant it, and that I hoped that each of them, fifty years after their deaths, would have something as utterly useless done for them. (Oscar Wilde tells us that all art is useless, but one must examine his meaning thoughtfully.) So, with a classmate who had come to hear me, I planted the tree, and doing this made me happy.

After these small musings I walk through Harvard Yard and wonder where I would look for God on this campus. Those vain academics were only looking for themselves: tenured insecurity. My place, my private corner where I sensed whatever God attended me, was in my old corner seat in the spacious vaulted reading room of Widener Library. That was the visiting room, for me, of the angels I knew then. John Coolidge played a part in that too, a star part. He pulled strings—academic tassels—and procured for me a card to the stacks when I was a sophomore, a privilege given usually only to juniors and seniors. I could pass through the small door behind the main desk and drift through the vast and crowded and dim low-ceilinged stacks and find the books I wanted in their intimacy, rummaging for them in their bedrooms instead of waiting for delivery in an outer room after a cold and formal search through the card catalogues. You never knew whom you might find curled up in there next to your choice. Those books, those thrills, were the sunny spring-green foliage of my boyhood, because in college I was still a boy.

The clearing! Yes, that's what it was! To be in the clearing, the great reading room. To face in the direction—that small door, the gateway. The magic words, the words needed for entry? My boyhood, my desire to learn. And the miracles I sought? My angels, the books. Now, the clearing is still there, the direction in which to face is still there. Ah, the magic words? Can I now, a white-haired man who gets into the movies at reduced cost, do I have any magic words left? Can I get a miracle? If I can recall my youth and understand it, that may be the miracle I seek now.

I believed in those angels, they were the writers, the painters, the composers when I went as a boy from the clearing into their presence. Perhaps they walk with me in a life that has been fortunate, and maybe they are from a mysterious and central force. But I know also that I made them come to me, not by a pious or moral life but because I sought them, and that restless seeking is my gift from my mother ("Nothing you couldn't do, David") and a few of my teachers in high school, and Helen Merrill and "Pop" LaRue are names I always want to mention.

Perhaps my angels came from here, from this college where I arrived feeling inadequate because I believed that my father pulled strings, another kind, to get me in. That feeling didn't last past the first five minutes, after meeting some of my classmates. But there was magic here, and there still is for me. Now we can fast-forward only a few months to another event that takes place here. It starts when our class reunion book arrives. There were not so many of us, perhaps a thousand, and it's easy to skim through looking for familiar names. Some of the dullest have written the longest biographies. Almost all claim the sunniest of lives, and their writing is like those Christmas family letters so often filled with names like Binky or Boo. I was not that active socially and instead spent many hours each day as an apprentice at the Brattle Theatre, but in the class book I recognize many of the names, and many of them are printed in the lighter, italicized typeface that is reserved for the dead. Among the still living is a friend, Dave Lee, who was quiet and bespeckled in that withdrawn scholarly way, such a nice kid, a hard worker in physics, sometimes trying to explain to us concepts that excited him. Dave didn't have an abundance of small talk. He was gentle and of course vulnerable, and almost invisible at a party. I sought him out in the dining hall because you could sit with him and talk or not talk. We were friends, and he had others, and enough, but he was not what we called a B.M.O.C. His biography is short, just wife and children and grandchildren, his work continues in the Department of Physics at Cornell, and then the shortest of comments: "Awarded the 1996 Nobel Prize. . . ." I guess you don't have to say a lot more. The Nobel Prize! Good grief! Here I am, trying to be a bar mitzvah, and Dave wins the Nobel!

I write, just saying "HOLY SHIT" in big letters, and "That was you!" and I can't resist asking what took him so long.

In my own biographical sketch I tried to be amusing, and I wrote that I taught a course at the college as my twenty-fifth reunion gift, and it was made clear to me that the class committee would have preferred the money. I served on a special committee of the Board of the Overseers. We reviewed the teaching of theater, and were called the Committee to Visit the Loeb. The Loeb is the name of the theater, and as a student I had organized a rally that helped to create it. Now, our committee worked hard enough, and we had a few famous members, such as Lillian Hellman and Robert Anderson, and we wrote reports that used words like "seriatum." Then President Bok—desiring, or so we believed, to get the maintenance cost of the theater building and its activities off his back—invited a well-known acting company to inhabit the building, to mop the floors, take out the garbage, and perform. They would teach students as a spin-off. Bok did this without asking for our learned humphs, so we all resigned. My letter stated that my only regret was that I didn't have more to resign from. I probably said "more from which to resign."

I wish I needed to write as little as Dave Lee wrote.

"Nothing you couldn't do," I hear my mother say. Sure, Mom.

I am overjoyed. I am thrilled when I learn ways in which people I care for are noted or remembered. I have the recent handsome and informative memorial book about Norman Geschwind, who was headed toward a Nobel had he lived on. But a Nobel for which of his achievements? If you asked Norman for the time, three hours later a new interdisciplinary field of medicine was established, and you hadn't needed to say a word. Then there are national awards for my friends Jacques D'Amboise and Eddie Villella.

Other enticing news in the class book, and I'm sure that many of us turned to it immediately and eagerly, is the current status report of one classmate. In our fortieth anniversary book, five years ago, he wrote an electrifying report, and here are some bits of it: "Saturday night. . . . I had been off the bottle for about ten days when I suffered from a hallucination involving my long-dead father. . . . I picked up a hunting knife and stabbed my mother [exactly at this point he interrupted the narrative to give us in parenthesis her full three names, the last her maiden name, and the name of her Ivy League college, with her year of graduation] in the heart, killing her with a single stab wound." He then described, and he wrote powerfully, his trials in both the legal and the broad sense. Not all was easy, including the mandated psychiatric care, where "the psychiatrist turned out to be a real cocksucker. . . ." He missed our twenty-fifth, being at that time in prison. He reported that he was in "the twelve-step program for those of us who have an insatiable propensity for imbibing spirits, which I demonstrated sufficiently in college. . . . I am sure, deep down, that I believe in God and have joined the Presbyterian Church." He talked of foraging in Dumpsters, but finally he took a job as a paralegal (before the fatal Saturday night he was a full legal) and now he had "my own office with bookcase, windows, desk, and telephone." I'm sure there was a chair—shades of my Uncle Eddie. Our classmate looked forward to our fiftieth reunion, but now, in this forty-fifth report, perhaps advised by a new psychiatrist, he only lists his address, so we'll have to wait for more news. His name is sonorous and Old Boy, with a "Jr."

Reunions are always the same and always different. Perhaps my idea, that the repentant man will be the keynote speaker at our fiftieth, will catch on. In answer to this, the phrase "I should live so long," or its gentile equivalent, is heard much, and at a dignified service in the old King's Chapel in Boston we hear the names of our class dead read simply, Vietnam wall–style. About a quarter of us are accounted for in this way. Leonora and I arrive late and find pews in the gallery next to the organist, and I'm far more taken by the beautiful movement of his feet on the pedal board than by the matter at hand. "You're not chopped liver, young man," I say to him at the end.

Dave Lee is at the party with his handsome and commonsensical wife, Dana, who seems to be fully capable of pointing him in the right direction in daily matters. We hug and then he stands with his arms spread and quietly says, looking at the roomful, "How delightful to see all of my old friends."

Others come to him, and I hear Dave admit to one that he is not so smart. "Well, smarter than me—er—than I?" is the apt rejoinder. So we finally sit and talk. He still sails, and he bought and enjoyed the book I wrote with my son and we have ordinary things to chatter about. He mentions my letter. "I enjoyed it," he says. "Very spontaneous." He's been speaking since the award, although I never would have envisioned Dave as a public speaker. I cannot fill in the years since I knew him: his personal life or the classes that he thoughtfully taught, so I want to hear him. He had recently given the commencement address at the University of Connecticut, only an hour down the road, but I didn't know about it. The fearful thing about the award ceremony in Stockholm, says Dave, was that he'd heard he might have to dance with the Queen of Sweden. Dave the dancer is not in my Technicolor picture of him—nor his: he took dancing lessons. "Lessons for Laureates" could be a catchy ad. Then there was a change in the style of the ceremony, and no one danced with the Queen.

Dave's modesty is to be expected from him and is refreshing, but he is deeply delighted and knows in his heart that he is deserving, and this is where a good wife helps a quiet man. A few times he uses the word "laureate" instead of "winner," and the pretty word blossoms.

I see that he walks the same way—how the picture leaps back! He doesn't shuffle, though my mother and probably his would bark out, "Lift your feet!" He slants toward the right as into a stiff northeast breeze and his head is down, his eyes fiercely intent on a moving point on the ground about eight feet ahead.

And then something happens to me that I may pleasantly struggle to explain to myself for the rest of my life. Dave and Dana go off, and I start to cry. Leonora and I are sitting at a table with eight others, our plastic plates emptied of the usual buffet fare. On the table is a big basket of peanuts, because some clever caterer realized that Old Boys like them and we might think we're at the Dartmouth Game. I don't care that others are watching me over the scattered shells. Leonora sees me and in a flash her hand is softly on my arm, and I blubber, "I'm so pleased, I'm so pleased, I'm so pleased, I'm so pleased."

Can the discovery of Superfluid He^3 create tears like this? Of course it can and why not and what better? Does the award-winning achievement have to be that of one's child or spouse or closest friend? Apparently not, apparently not. Do public tears have to be only in my old line of work, the death of Mimi in Act IV? (Light cue 83, if I remember accurately.) Apparently not, apparently not.

But why cry, really, why say "I'm so pleased?" Maybe this has more importance than I can realize. I've never had a less complicated moment in my life. Moments of great passion, of course, moments of achievement, as when a curtain went down and the audience was too touched to applaud; moments with Leonora and my children and the birth of grandchildren; looking at the rock itself, Cape Horn, from a tiny boat with my son. The usual moments that are silly yet profound, worthy and not. Why a moment of joy, now, for another, that surpasses my own? For me, there was always something else in the mix. Moments of all kinds are complex. They are tempered with pride, even exaltation, with hope for the future, or with some tiny embellishment built in to the moment. Not here. For almost the first time in my life my mind felt emptied of everything except that one emotion.

I know that big moments can come along quietly and in plainly wrapped packages. Big things pass by in dim corners, or too distant and not perceived, or too faintly sensed at a moment when our eyes are directed to another rustle in the forest. Maybe I did catch this, maybe this is the moment that I didn't expect and don't feel confident that I deserve. Maybe, just maybe, my thoughts, my few studies, my hopes, and my life itself, so erratic but now calming, have peeled back another layer. Maybe I can sit with my mind emptied except for pleasure at a triumph that is not mine, and maybe my very own sense of God has sent down this root, in surprisingly innocent simplicity. Maybe I'm blessed by the sharpened ability to recognize such a moment. Maybe that is enough, and maybe one day I'll understand it. Maybe, in order to understand it, I must realize that there's nothing more to understand.

Of course there's an old and wise way to see this, and Doug offers a thought to me just before the next class. Rabbi Menahem Mendel of Kotsk simply called this kind of happening an act of selflessness, meaning the rare moment when ego is not in play. This man, known alarmingly as "the Kotsker," also pointed out that everything in the world can be imitated except truth, because truth, once imitated, is no longer truth. And he said that God dwells wherever man lets Him in. Maybe I let God in, for a fleeting moment, there on the Starlight Roof of some overrated Boston hotel, where suddenly time stopped or slowed down. Maybe I'm getting the idea.

Chapter 20

✳   ✳   ✳

THE END OF THE AFFAIR

A SMALL ALMOST-MIRACLE is happening. Just as I seem to be running out of memory cells to store Hebrew, I'm starting to sight-read. I'm starting to see and sound out, at a slow but steady pace, the words. I've been doing this, to be sure, but like a first grader, yanking out a word at a time, going back over sixty years to that jerky way of early readers. See—Spot—run. Now it's starting to smooth out, and in the nick of time indeed. I won't have to memorize, I'll be able to read on the bema.

In my Merlin life I suddenly recall my favorite book as a child, and possessing it again becomes an obsession. Not for me, oh no, could I be that selfish? No, for my grandchildren, never mind that they can sop up this information from the Internet, with movement and music. I recall the thin book with delight, I turn the pages in my mind and see each picture, I remember entire chunks of text. I phone the Library of Congress, and in only a few moments the book is found: *The Wonder World of Ants.* The author, forgotten by me, is Wilfrid S. Bronson, and what eight-year-old reads or remembers the publisher? Harcourt, Brace, 1937. I phone a book-finding company, and in less than two weeks, minus $60, I am reading it again, though not lying on my stomach the way kids do. My memory was accurate. I remember the pictures, and as I turn the pages, now delicate, I know what colored or black-and-white drawing will be on the next page. Yes, that mustache, on the terrified man who has placed the four legs of his bed in pails of kerosene as a million army ants course through his room. Will they crawl up the walls and drop on him from the ceiling? Good question. I remember the text accurately. "Great King Solomon urged his people to be more like the industrious ant." There also, to illustrate the chapter on Amazon ants, is a drawing of bare-chested human Amazons riding into battle. "*Un*-necessary," my mother would have said had she seen it, but it was natural, she would have reasoned, and she wouldn't have burned the book. Thus nudity encourages scholarship in the young. We continue, "Since I could not go to Africa, I went out into the fields and lay with my eyes very close to the ground . . . I was not a boy watching ants but an explorer." Is it any wonder that I loved this book? Damned if those grandchildren are going to tear it apart. It's mine! I didn't have that many books as a kid, and I treasured each. I had all I could read, of course, but not more than that. My grandchildren have thousands of dollars' worth of Lego alone, and so many toys and games, quickly disposed of when they break, that I am frightened for their minds. Yet only a few weeks ago I was driving with Jesse, nine as I write this, and when I turned on the radio a violin melody grew in the car, and after only one measure I asked him what it was and without hesitation he said, "That's the Beethoven." Figure it out.

Another miracle. Leonora and I go south to visit our friends, now ill, and stay at an ocean-front hotel, a thin slab of a building stuck into the Florida beach, stretched north-south, all rooms facing the water. We are on the eleventh floor; the brisk wind is from the northeast but it deflects and races due south along the balconies of the façade. Pelicans fly in this corridor of wind. These are magnificent birds, big and graceful despite the pterodactyl head, and they present handsome detail in the scalelike edging color of their dark feathers. They have "jizz," the delightful term that birders use; it means "star quality." Attention-grabbing birds, silhouetted against the glare of the morning sun on the water as they parade, wings hardly moving. Right to left. My Hebrew letters, there, moving! Dark and solemn. Quiet, almost still in their passing, their lift is the strong head current, they use a full minute to pass our balcony. Their wingtips are about eight feet out, wings that spread seven feet. Each gazes at me like the Torah text, I feel my body lift, I could step out into the air and go with them, with my letters, The Law on vellum, now in the air. Slowly, slowly they gain distance, and about thirty feet to my left they raise their left wings slightly, slightly, and the wind is caught and they are lifted and spun and in a moment they sweep past me. Thirty feet to my right they turn again, but now the turn is into the wind and they pivot like slow turntables; a pin could center each seven-foot diameter. I can see the air! All my years knowing the wind, it is visible, as current.

Is there ever enough?

I think of my urge to step out into the visible air. I'm one of those who fear that they will throw themselves over a cliff or a railing into space, but this is always outdoors and selective; it never occurs to me on a theater balcony or when I'm clinging to the top of a mast. When I do become nervous, I remember the remark of

Edith Oliver, a superb critic of drama and most other things. I asked her if she felt this desire to throw herself off. She said no, her thoughts were always of others she'd like to push. Edith's funny remark calms me when I'm on heights.

There is more. This beach is not perfect because it has patches of a rock named coquina, a limestone of solidified coral and seashells. The outcroppings are interesting and handsome above the tide line, but sharp and annoying when they rake you from their hiding places under the water. I don't like swimming; I'm a boater, and the whole point of expensive boats is, obviously, to keep you *out* of the water. But I swim from time to time and have good memories of Rockaway Beach. Now I can't resist a moonlight dip and yes, Mom, I wait an hour after my meal. I lose my balance in a small breaking wave and am rolled, not unpleasantly, along the bottom. I touch a rock and barely feel the contact, but later I can see blood on the towel, and in our room I deal with the cuts. A gash on my left instep, smaller cuts on my right and left palms. Good grief, the stigmata! Well, three-quarters of the stigmata, or three-fifths if you count the gash from the lance in Jesus' side. What did I do to deserve this? It comes from no fervor in the relevant direction. Nor is it spontaneous, which is vital, and not complete, which also counts heavily against canonization. So I rule it out as a sign from another camp. Darn, this is painful. Stigmata indeed. And my classmates have only to worry about zits.

Back home, more news-of-the-week reports, and one is stylish. "Rabbi, to make a long story short, my parakeet died." Then in class, "C'mon Alex, stop being an adolescent!" Doug speaks to us about slavery. Our slavery in Egypt was for four hundred years, not dissimilar to black slavery in this country. The point is that we escaped from Egypt. Black people stayed in the society that enslaved them. This reasoning appeals to the class. Convinced that they are slaves to the cruel wills of their parents, they see moving away as emancipation. I tell the story of my son wanting his own apartment when he was eleven. We were driving back into New York after a country visit, and our dog, a poor traveler, was with us. "Dan," I said, "look at your room! It's a shocking mess. How could you live by yourself?" and at that exact moment the dog leaned over and threw up in his lap. Then I'm sorry that I told the story. Outside, yes, but in class I'm not a parent with stories about his kids, and I'm not an assistant teacher. I'm a student.

We talk about lying, pro and con. As with all subjects, the Talmud presents many arguments about this, relating to saving lives. "There has been much rabbinical discussion." Don't open the Talmud to find black-and-white pronouncements. I tell of my friend Paul's death, which was not told to his mother, Rebecca, who was already fabulously old, 98–120. Why upset her? She wasn't taking in information, or so it seemed. But in a rare lucid moment, she said, "Soon I'll be with my beloved Herman and with my son Paul." It was mystical and frightened those who had tried to fool her.

We sit on cushions in another room for Hebrew class. My classmates are off like a shot, or shots, at the close of the class. I'm not even struggling to my feet as yet; I'm sitting there trying to devise a way to struggle to my feet. Slaves my foot, these kids.

Alex becomes a bar mitzvah. Our first, and he is excellent. A full house, about 120 in our synagogue. Alex stands steady as a rock and is fluent and clear, he knows his stuff. Doug announces my help and thanks me for it. He had asked me to listen to the sermons, not so much for content but for presentation. Most of my classmates ask for my help, or are talked into it, and I'm flattered. Usually the call comes from the mother, and we meet at the synagogue with Doug a few days before the ceremony in the late afternoon, when Doug will review the sermon. I explain to the kids that I'm not there for Hebrew or religious expertise, they're better than I am, but I've spent fifty years looking at presentations by actors, and I want to help only in that way. The advice is simple and they all need it: first, push the written-out sermon away from you on the reading stand, as far away as you can comfortably see the writing. That will lift your face toward the audience. Second, keep your feet still! We can see under the reading stand and will be fascinated with knee bumping and ankle crossing if you're not nailed down. Relax and shift a bit, sure, but between prayers and sections. The girls are more jiggly than the boys. I suggest to Doug that we could put a facing on the bema, and that could cover a trap door.

Alex seemed pleased by the advice. There are one or two words that I didn't hear clearly. I note those, and Doug and I suggest a different construction when the sentence is a tongue-knotter. My classmates' sermons will all be bold and fun. Doug lets them have their say. Alex speaks of his soccer as a metaphor for life. Play hard, respect teammates, never be discouraged.

On his big day, Alex has dozens of grandparents, uncles, aunts, and cousins who go up to the bema to recite a blessing, which they can read in Hebrew, or from the English transliteration of Hebrew, or in English. These are called "honors" or "aliyahs," the sense is of journey, and are done by anyone over thirteen in our congregation, you don't have to be Jewish. In our congregation in another part of the ceremony, after Alex has completed his various prayers, blessings and passages in Hebrew—about nine and of varying lengths—the congregation throws candy at him to show the sweetness of it all. Doug emphasizes "adults only" when he describes the process, but the kids all sneak candy from the baskets that are passed around, and they fire with a will and good aim. A Tootsie Roll or a Hershey's Kiss can sting. By the time we're ready for the toss I've eaten mine.

The party is at a restaurant alongside the Connecticut River. Alex's younger brother is learning saxophone and takes two turns with the small band; not bad. I try to sit for a moment with the kids, but suddenly they lift off and race somewhere. Then Leonora and I sit with Doug and my teacher Debbie, and we learn that Doug took five years at "rabbi school'"—the phrase he likes—after two years of Hebrew at Wesleyan University. A bald eagle lives in a tree across the river, and we watch him dive to its surface.

The ice is broken with this first bar mitzvah. My classmates are excited for themselves and happy for Alex, and no one seems terrified, except me. There was a caring atmosphere on the bema and that is encouraging, and they feel they're learning their stuff and will be ready. Leonora starts in with me about the party. I wish I were a kid and was told to not worry, Mom and Dad will take care of it. This is going to be a Leonora perfection-worry ordeal.

On Sunday, May 4th, we are all in class except Alex. The work moves ahead soberly and directly. We prepare a service for Yom Ha-Shoah, remembrance of the Holocaust. All cooperate. I give a short sermon stating that when all of the Holocaust witnesses are dead—people my age and only ten years younger—then perhaps we'll have a new world and can regain our religion based on who we are and what we believe and do, rather than on what other people did to us. And I sing the *Ani Ma' Amin* prayer well enough, not brilliantly, but this is a good experience. I want to sing my pieces carefully, not race along like my classmates with only an occasional sense of a musical note. Not that I'm complaining, I should do so well, I quickly add for the benefit of the mal-angels perched on my shoulders.

Poor Rabbi Doug, he gets it from all sides. He tells me that little Billy, a class below me and so smart, came up to him after my sermon and said that it was about time that someone in the school said something sensible.

Then, at the end of May, our next-to-last class. "I sprained my ankle, Rabbi." "I hit in the winning run." I fight off telling them about my friend Dave Lee who won the Nobel Prize.

We write an essay in class. Debbie is concerned that I don't spend too much time on it. After all, my *Anne Frank* was eight weeks late. She reminds me of my poetry disaster. We were to write short poems describing each of the important prayers we were studying. All of my classmates had finished their poems and tiptoed out. I hadn't noticed and sat alone in the classroom, staring at the ceiling, still trying to decide which form I would use. Doggerel? Limerick? Haiku? Today my subject is the Warsaw ghetto. She brings me a source book and shows me how to adapt a few paragraphs, and it takes me only a half hour. Then we work on books, lettering our condensed main prayers and gluing on the covers we made months ago. Adam, whose bar mitzvah is this Saturday, is alert and helpful. When I lose something, he is instantly at my side. That's his nature, and he hides it under cool indifference. Well, Doug said they'd shape up before their ceremonies. Adam had to wait until the very last minute, of course. Everyone in class is helpful, except Jami. Debbie asks her about her morning blessings—what do you bless for? Nothing, she says.

We phone Rebecca Price, our teacher who has taken a work-trip to Israel, and the whole school listens and questions are asked. Where do you live, have you fired a rifle, how did you spend the charity money we collected for you to hand out?

In our last Wednesday class, I hold the Torah for the first time, and I'm nervous. Then Doug tells us that he has learned that some of the Durham kids have been passing notes saying terrible things about their teachers. The notes are in English, but using Hebrew letters. So we construct sentences using a technique like this, but we use real Hebrew words from our prayers, words that could also mean "he's a hunk," etc. Adam, again a mensch, is my partner.

After my tutorial, Sara's mom tells me that Sara has doubts about her readiness for the ceremony, certainly not about her Hebrew skills, and her mom told her that the readiness had to be in the heart, and Sara cried, and she is ready. That's really good mom advice. Then she told Sara that she's going to feel transformed when Doug puts his arm around her on the bema. Mom says that the ceremony is a passage for the whole family. What will it be for me? Just another of my oddball adventures? I ask about the gift I can buy Sara. She's interested in nail polish, boys, music. I know nothing about nail polish. Boys? A search committee? Forget that. Music it will be, a gift certificate from Record Town. That's my gift to most of the kids, but I give to Aaron a video of *Captains Courageous,* and to Mark, at his request, signed copies of books I've written. It occurs to me that all they really want at this age is a lock for their bedroom doors. A better gift and cheaper.

Leonora says, "You did fine, those are irreparable gifts."

I drive down to Manhattanville College, in Purchase, for an event, and park by a glowing Ireland-green field. A baby bird is taking its first flight, under a crab-apple tree. The nest must be in the tree. He flutters and can make progress. A dog appears, so black against the brilliant green that it is only the silhouette of a dog, a black cut-out, the way Manet and Degas throw black at us. The shocking profile, active and excited, races across the field, and I transform the manicured trees to the forest in *Peter and the Wolf.* The dog is too far away to see the bird, which manages to fly to a foot-grip on the tree trunk about three feet up, halfway to the first branch. He or she pauses, and even from my distance, perhaps twenty feet, I can see the little chest heaving. Then I see a mature bird, surely a parent, watching from the branch.

Suddenly I am involved. The chick flies at my pickup, trips on the upper edge of the bed and tumbles in. I watch in the rearview mirror. He's panting and his childish feathers are a messy fluff. He tries to fly up out of the bed and fails twice. Now the parent, dapper and calm, perches encouragingly on the bed rim, then flies to the lawn on the other side. The juvenile flutters again and fails again. I'll have to help unless I want to raise a bird in the back of my truck. I open the door and step out. The birdlet gasps and cowers and hops, tripping and tumbling twice, to the far side of the truck bed. Am I a frightening sight? I smooth down my hair, I turn my sweater so that the hole at the base of the turtle-neck can't be seen, and I smile. I realize too late that only carnivores smile. With a *kvitch* the little fellow launches a flight and now, using the full length of the bed, his low angle of rise is sufficient and he clears the tailgate like Lindbergh clearing the wires. He's already pointed in the exact direction of the waiting father or mother on the far lawn. Astonishing. The little flier sets his or her flaps and glides and flutters at a long, shallow angle and lands by the parent. True as a dart. A pause, and together they skim at elevation two feet to a thick bush and are out of sight.

By tomorrow or the next day this bar-mitzvah bird will be a

nonchalant teenager, his feathers finished and elegantly combed. But think about it, only three or four weeks ago this little fellow was an egg! In the tiny head is complex knowledge waiting for its time: how to choose a mate that is exactly his species amongst the dozens of subtly differentiated finches, how to build a nest and raise hatchlings, and then how to worry about their first flight. Did I know that much without being taught? Actually, yes: walking is complicated, so is talking, and these seem to be built-ins to my species. But who cannot admire this bird youngster?

On Saturday, Adam is splendid at his bar mitzvah, but one relative, on the bema for his honor, keeps a hand in his pocket and two others chew gum. The positioning is such that Doug could not see them. I squirm. My theater training obliges me to keep shows neat and focused. When one actor speaks, the others don't usually chew. I do not comment out loud as my mother might have done nor, like some of my magnificent spinster teachers in grade school, do I stride to the little stage and hold out my palm at chin level. But the ceremony is a tribute to Adam and his mother, who assembled the broken family in his honor.

One should keep a low profile during the ceremonies of others, but that's not always the case. When Leonora and I were being married the rabbi went on and on, stuff about artists being united. I regretted that we'd told him anything about ourselves. There was a roaring in my ears, and Leonora's shoulders were shaking from giggles. My mother was hard of hearing, so her voice could be loud, and no one in the room missed her appeal to my father: "Mortimer, isn't there some way we can make him stop?"

On Sunday we have our last Books and Bagels gathering, featuring an author in our congregation, Amy Bloom, and she is authoritative and attentive to questions. Then I race to the annex for the last day of class and to watch the DJ dancing, a switch from the usual school-end picnic. I'm chewed out mildly for my absence by our principal, who is perhaps fifteen years younger than I am, and I weakly explain that I was at work on a committee. In Amy's brilliant novel that we just discussed, her *Love Invents Us,* one character joins a synagogue and prays quietly in the rear until they find her and put her on a committee.

The school party gains some headway, and finally most of the kids, at least most of the girls, are jumping up and down on their little bird legs and doing the stylish arm gestures. My Young Lady is among them.

In the Kabbalah, the book of mysticism and secret doctrine, we learn that when Eliezer, the servant of Abraham, discovered Rebecca at the well, he was able with an incantation to make his camels rise into the air with himself elevated above them. Neat trick, attention-getting to the young woman. But where could I rent the camels? The message of the legend is twofold. First, impress the girl. Second, remember that Eliezer is an intermediary, in this case a double intermediary, sent by Abraham but on behalf of Isaac. Recalling the shyness of twelve or thirteen years of age, I see again the miserable devices. What would I have done? What do I remember about this painful time of life? Messages carried, notes in class, signed or unsigned letters, phone calls with a mysterious hang-up, giggling girls who somehow found out, eye contact or not (with or without puppy eyes), courses set to intersect on the school paths, and when all is lost, appear with a fake beard, and if she doesn't laugh, she isn't good enough for you—the way Leonora wasn't good enough for her father, yes, blame her.

At the party, Mark shows me a photograph of their class eight years ago. There is Jami, her lips pressed together tightly, a grimace of a smile, the smile that my son used for photographs at that age. I find Jami and show her the picture. "Do you remember how you felt when that was taken?" "Yes. Embarrassed." Yes, uncomfortable inside, wearing the smile-mask.

I watch the dancing, I look at the whipping ponytail of My Young Lady. What if this was class and Rabbi Doug called on me? Here I am, a thousand miles away, no, farther, because as Tennessee Williams tells us, time is the longest distance between two places, and I am ten thousand miles from twelve, but close, close, to my feelings then.

I guess the whole matter isn't going anywhere. So, so, so be it. She made an old man sing, or at least chirp, so be it.

I want to stay alive, suddenly this desire grips me so strongly that it jolts me: the ponytail. I promised Jordan a special trip when he is ten, three years from now. "Sure, Poppa, sure, if you live that long." He feels cheated by the death of his other grandfather, Aaron. He understands that life is brittle and the thought frightens him.

Doug tells me that one of the official closing ceremonies was to pass around the Torah and for each student to speak briefly. When it was his turn, Ben said that he knew he was a troublemaker, and he thanked his teacher for being so patient. "You know, Doug," I say, "there's a special and beautiful quality about Ben." Doug turns to me and smiles.

Chapter 21

*　*　*

CRANKY WITH THEE

I AM AGING without grace, a cranky man. My old God tells me that I can be cranky. He was, after all, and He lost His temper a few times. He forgives, if we ask. Some few people with a newer God, who is not cranky, go out and shoot people in His name. Some people don't like me because I'm not as holy as they are in just their way. I don't dislike anyone who has a different idea about "holy." I simply dislike assholes, and this is interfaith and with no regard for the color or shape of their skins, and often enough includes me. I don't have to apologize for disliking some people, or for being cranky. Given our wits, do we just stand around and smile when we're abused? That would be fine if everyone suddenly took to that belief, if all of us who seek individual self-enlightenment through Eastern techniques, or group enlightenment through any religion, did it all at once. In the meantime, imagine changing from British left-hand driving to the American right-hand style—gradually. Does God expect no volunteers down here? I'll give you some small examples of crankiness. Yes, small. I've done enough big things. Now, like my friend Mack Scism, I can say, "I've had enough ideas, I plan to live the rest of my life on my prejudices!" Or, to paraphrase Henry James, I can give myself the illusion of thinking by shuffling around my prejudices.

Yes, I went around Cape Horn in a tiny boat. "Sailor or landsman, there is some sort of a Cape Horn for all," says Melville. Did that make me a changed person? The young men who go to war and kill other men, or watch their friends meet death—are their own spared lives changed when they return? Rarely. The morning after we rounded the Horn, with terror and with my son, Dan, washed overboard briefly, he noted that he was glad his life was spared, but he was now furious because he couldn't get the little balls of Cremora to dissolve in his coffee. It is difficult to reset our built-in thermostats for tolerance or joy. Will I now carry on as an adversary to the world, as inherited from my mother? Will I do as she did, bringing up the alert rear of the march of progress? An amusing Yiddish word is *tsitser,* someone who sits around going tsist-tsist, or tsk-tsk, like that television philosopher. No, I want to act, and now I'm willing to wind up on a local level. The trick is to choose your small battles carefully and one at a time, and blaze away with humor. I'm busy and I give this only an hour each week. I raise my small lance and charge, but at one windmill at a time, and I usually win. Keeps the blood circulating.

The world isn't worse than it was. People have always been cheated and lied to, and with less recourse than we have today. Was there a lemon law in Dickens' time? There is now, and when General Motors tried to defraud me of my warranty, the State of Connecticut stepped in and collected for me, from GM, what I had paid a good mechanic to fix my Chevy. Messrs Goodwrench had been unable to locate or fix the flaw, and their bosses, at corporate level, had ingeniously claimed that I'd vandalized my car.

My friend Gene Lasko said, "I knew he wasn't a good mechanic. When he bent over you couldn't see his crack."

The fun of it was to request from the local fire department a permit to burn the Chevy in public. This was refused, but it was a good news item.

My latest one-hour-a-week job was to change something done by our post office. They ripped up perfect sidewalks and replaced them to conform to new wheelchair-ramp laws. The old reserved parking spot was near the front door, but is now moved to the distant last space in the lot. I talked to the architects, and they rationalized their decisions on the basis of ramp slopes, drainage, the maximum 2 percent slope under your car when it discharges the wheelchair, etc. Meticulous, but counter to the spirit of the law. There are three better ways to solve the problem, all cheaper, all meeting the new codes, and all close to the front door. But—redo the work? The architect himself finally made the suggestion. Now we have a sign stuck in at the good old parking place, where it belongs, and it states PARKING RESERVED FOR ELDERLY AND SPECIAL NEEDS. Not stylish grammatically and not official, but effective. A newspaper article cited me for compassion toward the disabled. Like hell it was, it was pure anger.

I do a minor job representing God on this earth, but shucks, someone has to. "Your complaint makes a difference" could be my fourth commandment.

I'm even cranky about love. On my answering machine: "Sorry, wrong number. I love you (click)." Why am I offended? Am I an unloving person, and therefore my reaction addresses the man's impertinence? I know that in my old profession we call people "dear" and "darling," and perhaps more than others we sign our letters "Love." That's ritual. The real stuff is tougher, it starts with respect.

One of our actresses fell in with another group, and when it came time for her to rejoin us for a foreign tour she insisted on staying with them. We had a valid contract and won her back, but I was chastised by the other producer. "David, you don't understand love. When a company member of mine wants to leave me, even just before a tour, I say to them that I love them, they should follow their heart." I replied that I loved the impresarios who had traveled from Europe to see us and had worked hard to bring us to their festivals, and I loved the audiences that they had lined up, and I wanted to give them our best. I loved my company and didn't want to pull them in from needed time off. The costly rehearsals necessary to replace this key actress would allow no loving bonuses this year. Again, *respect* is the forgotten word, and then love may grow.

I feel the pressure of my upcoming event. How silly, at this age, with a lifetime of deadlines and crises behind me. I'm torn between the fast track and this return to a slower life and ancient beliefs. I'm restless. And cranky. I'm cross today because I was experimenting with this time of my life, attempting to nap for a half hour after lunch. The "country," I am discovering, is like a hospital—no place to rest. Lawn mowers, tractors, the howl from the nearby volunteer fire station, the clatter of rain, the branches scraping on the roof, the crickets. Maybe the only place to rest in the civilized world is in the heart of a city. The city hums; the sirens and jackhammers are its blended and orchestrated sound, restful in the back bedroom.

It is late summer, the leaves have not begun to fall, but a few are down, victims of wind more than of their age or the season. In the parking lot of the condominiums across the street, an area for thirty cars that is perhaps ninety feet square, sixty or seventy leaves are scattered. They are pale yellow-green dots on the macadam. The parking lot plays a role in my life: it's where I fetch up if I slide down my driveway in winter. Or I back into it to get a drag-race start up the slant when the plow doesn't show up. It belongs to friends, Bill and Pat Kotchen, and often Bill, with a smile and a shrug, will plow my driveway when the snow has finished falling. Like many executives, he loves to work machinery and plow, the way I'd love to sit and work the levers on a tiny backhoe owned by another neighbor, a brilliant journalist. I visited him one day when he was sitting on that device, and he proudly pointed to the long narrow ditch behind him. "I've dug in two hours what two men would have done in a day." "Great, Morley," I say. "But why'd you dig it?" A thoughtful pause. "Because it wasn't there."

The roar that wakes me today is quickly explained. Three large and obviously strong men have set upon the leaves across the street and the battle is on. Harnessed to their backs are small, snarling gas engines with tubes attached that can be manipulated and aimed in a relaxed fashion at arm's length, reminiscent of more peaceful scenes at the urinals. But these men-engines are spewing jets of air to move the leaves. This is war, and they are knights with lances. Here a leaf shoots away from the champion. Here is a leaf in a tiny puddle, but soon the puddle is spattered and then, in time, the leaf is dried out and skitters away. Less than a minute for that one stubborn leaf. Nor does any single leaf withstand the attack. Take that! There are clutches on the machines and they snarl in different times and raucous harmonies. Engage! Disengage! Action! These must be four-horsepower engines, and I see twelve magnificent war horses in jousting regalia, rearing and snorting and then charging.

The leaves are gathered in a corner of the lot. One man turns off his engine and starts for the truck, parked thirty yards away. Another stands alert at idle, perhaps guarding against a gust of wind. I hope for this, I want to see him spring in pursuit, perhaps leaping over the end-zone stripe to slap back a leaf with a gust of air, blow it back before his feet hit the ground out of bounds. Now the first man returns with a broom and dustpan, his engine still strapped to his back. He hands the dustpan to the other, who bends down. In a moment all of the leaves are fitted into the small dustpan, just one load, and with his free hand as a cover, the man walks back to his truck and dumps them into a metal drum. Then he turns off his engine. The others join him; they sit on the tail-gates and light up. Then they drive off in three separate pickup trucks.

A memory from Japan: a sudden silent haiku memory picture in snow, 1960 in Kyoto. An old, bent woman with a willow broom sweeps in quiet radii, slowly, the long graceful curves of scything rhythm.

Rights and wrongs, old ways, new ways. The bar mitzvah approaches. I try to put behind me the crime that cost me and my company so much: the lost jobs, the violated trust, a life's work entrusted, then traded for costly wines and debonair jackets. The nagging question is still with me. Someday, can I forgive? If not, does this mean that I am a small man? Yes, Ravenal is having his time in jail, yes, his defense at the sentencing was pathetic. Not without humor: at one point his attorney suggested that he do community service instead of jail time; that's funny because the company that he robbed is the very essence of community service. No one laughed, and I was disappointed. Then it was suggested that he not do jail time because his mother was old. She had

Alzheimer's and didn't recognize him—but hey, have a heart. This is funny because it echoes the joke about the man who murders his parents (in this case their legacies) and then throws himself on the mercy of the court because he's an orphan.

Leonora said, "Half of what he made up wasn't even true."

Of course I've grown in the process. When the troubles started, I went on a diet of candy bars. Now, when I look down, I can't see beyond a promontory, a Buddha-belly. There is a Yiddish phrase for this. A rough translation would be "Mirror-balls."

I go to Rabbi Doug. In my new life I am a peasant in the village, going to the rabbi for advice. Am I too stern, I ask? Should I turn the other cheek, the way New Testament people should? But their ways can be confusing. Loathe the crime, love the criminal.

Understanding our penal laws, I've been told, and now question, with Doug, is like reading a sacred text. You can read it as history and culture—what it has to say about the past, with all its imperfections and injustices and cultural biases—or you can read it as an attempt to inspire action in the future, as a guide, a pointer, a metaphor or analogy or example of Right. Like my mother, Doug can find his way to the center of the argument and comfort me. Our tradition, he says, calls for restitution. "First restitution, then forgiveness." This I understand, and I can wait. At Ravenal's $500 per month of restitution (with interest, Doug adds, that's our ancient way), that's a lot of years. Add the money he never paid to my friends and the raises we couldn't give and the jobs lost. At my age then, when I'm closing in on 120, if this is done and he understands what he did, I will forgive. Yes, I tell Doug, he can then sit anytime at my table.

Doug tells me about the Rebukers, itinerant rabbis who traveled from town to town in Eastern Europe, particularly in the early nineteenth century. They were hired to administer deserved rebukes. So, Schlomo the Rebuker would rebuke a man or a whole congregation, but three standards had to be met. Both the employer and the rebuker had to examine his own heart, and if the motivation was personal hatred, Schlomo would not rebuke. Second, the rebuke was to make the offender change, not just to punish him. Finally, was the rebuker guilty of the same thing before rebuking another for it? I see Schlomo as a cranky man. I'd like to try his job.

> *Do what you will, this life's a fiction*
> *And is made up of contradiction.*
> —William Blake

> *You have to see it from both sides of the speculum.*
> —Leonora Hays

Chapter 22

✻ ✻ ✻

I READ THE LAW

DURING AUGUST AND SEPTEMBER I study for two hours every day with care and fright. In my mind are the smooth-as-silk performances of my classmates. All but Hannah and Mark, who will come after me, have succeeded well, each has said, "Today I am a Man (or Woman)," or had it said to them. I've received handsome thank-you notes from all for my small gifts. Adam added that I should not worry, it was easy, and his well-intentioned wish was the formal beginning of terror.

In high school I was involved and popular, president of this and that, captain of teams, and so forth. My grades were poor in some subjects, but my college board scores were at the top, so high in Latin, for example, that my teacher, none other than the poet and translator Rolphe Humphries, was called in by the headmaster to explain why the Princeton people thought so highly of me while he did not. The answer is in the multiple-choice test system. There was no way that I could remember a Latin word, but I could pick it out of the lineup with three other words and check the correct box. My mind has always seemed to work two feet below the surface. The stuff is there, but not on top. I need time, things come together and come out when they're ready. I could not make a fast-on-your-feet prosecuting attorney, following my father's eminent path. When we graduated from high school I was to give an address as salutatorian, an honor requiring election by the class, not the teachers. I wrote my speech and memorized it, as was our custom, and as I delivered it on a hot June day, next to a rented palm, I "went up," and there I stood, not a word in my mind. After about three days of mute standing, I mumbled something, such as "What I wanted to say before I forgot," and got a cheap laugh of relief from the agonized audience. I said my last line, which had come to me, and sat down in flaming-faced disgrace. The situation was made worse for me because I had worked for special honors in two subjects, but there had been some foul-up and neither was announced. Not a good day.

For years after that day I couldn't address a group. Then slowly I began again, but I vowed never to memorize. Nor do I enjoy reading from a prepared sheet, because I sound stilted. Wandering from a fully written speech can make it difficult to find my way back: as I fight to the surface from my off-the-cuff footnotes and ad-libs I can lose my verb or worse in the process. So I make an outline and improvise from that. It sounds fresh and it is. I have to be alert, yet I'm not frightened. But I'm frightened now.

When I return home, there is a letter waiting, addressed in familiar handwriting: mine. I open it and remember that a year ago almost to the day, on September 11, 1996, I wrote this note to myself in Hebrew school, answering three questions that were dictated to the class by Doug. It's been held by the school for the year and now mailed to me. The questions: "What will you be thinking of on the day of your bar mitzvah?" "What will you be hoping on that day?" "If you had one wish for yourself on that day, what would it be?"

My first answer is foolishly formal, but not bad: "I will be thinking of friends and family no longer living, and of my grandchildren, who are." Quite a span of generations. To the good, the grandchildren will all attend the ceremony, and that includes ten-year-old Stephan, now Dan's stepson by marriage, all of which had not yet been decided a year ago. Others? My father's and mother's names are on the plaque on the synagogue wall near the bema, and on the anniversaries of their deaths we screw in their candle bulbs, and we will do that for this big day. Doug will also read out the name of Jack's father, Aaron, at the ceremony, and Rebecca and Paul Shulman's names.

My second answer, a year in advance, is my best. "Simply that I don't make a fool of myself."

I explain this to Doug. I'll be singing the text, so I have the tune and the words to deliver. If one loses the tune, the words fall apart. My classmates memorize the Hebrew, realizing that it's easier than learning to read at delivery speed from the page or scroll. The written text launches them into each section, to be sure, but then they know it by heart. I'm too old to memorize, and as I've written above, I was never much good at it. So I have to read and sing, and I'm nervous that suddenly I'll be looking at strange shapes on vellum with a flat line showing on my brain monitor. Doug says don't worry, I'll be fine. Maybe he knows something that I don't yet know, maybe he's been told of certain magic powers. I'll come to that.

My third answer is expressed in a schoolboyish and awkward

way, the deathless-prose department. "That what I have gained will live with me in strength for the rest of my life." Okay. But how long will that be? After my bypass operation, I said to my mother that she might outlive me. "Sure," she said, "by five minutes."

I try to concentrate as I study, but there's always a leaky gasket somewhere, and other thoughts streak in and out. I feel only 50 percent sealed off from the world as I study. But that's how my mind works, it races. That may be good for getting artistic concepts, which must weave many strands at great speed and come together at the "*Aha!*" The exceptions to my scatter-mindedness in recent years are so few that I can remember each: during Joseph Campbell's lectures fifteen years ago (live, not on TV), and Rabbi Doug's Bible classes today, and my way of meditating when I sail. I can be totally lost in a film, though this applies rarely to TV or to a play, where I am prone to visits by that special angel we all share from birth, the Angel of Sleep. In a few days, will I be able to focus when I'm on the bema?

The arrangements have been made. I was too impatient to order invitations and instead bought handsome cards and wrote by hand. Bar mitzvahs today can cost much, and here is a newspaper feature telling us that bar mitzvahs rarely cost under $15,000 and often go for over $90,000. I assume that this does not reflect Orthodox custom. The picture shows a thirteen-year-old boy whose eyes are nipple height, and he is gazing at two of these very things at his party. Maybe the exotic dancer was doing a relevant Mediterranean dance, perhaps the Dance of the Seven Veils. Our party will be at Chester's beautiful Old Meeting House, a small theater with a deliciously curved balcony in which Lincoln would have been proud to be shot. We'll feature simple good deli food, like hot pastrami, and our band, A Klez Act, will play. I've bought jackets for them, making one of Cookie's dreams come true. We'll dance.

This is the last time I'm going to become a bar mitzvah without my mother. She might have been as nervous as Leonora, but her thirteen-year-old-son would not know that. Leonora indeed carries on to perfection as always, but with worry and energy that swamp me. The party arrangements are the big seas, and my small boat is tossed about as I overhear phone call after phone call: who's coming? will they stay overnight? will there be hors d'oeuvres? a call to Rabbi Doug because we can't eat until after the blessing over the meal, but it will take the family too long to get to the party if we stay a moment for pictures, and people will be hungry or start to eat. Doug says that we will do the blessing over the bread in the synagogue. We'll stand around the piano (our biggest table) and sip a bit of the wine, and that will answer the requirement. On and on. Rita Thorpe is our extraordinary food overseer at The Theatre of the Deaf and she's catering this, but Leonora can be relentless when she runs a party or a fund drive.

She's not been well this winter: "I have a condition that's been exasperated by these drugs." But a party looms and she's back on top.

It is time. Julia and Jack and their three children arrive Friday afternoon, and our friend Doug May will pick up Dan and Wendy and Stephan at the Hartford airport after their flight from Idaho. I start tonight during services with two of the big prayers, the V'Ahavta and the Avot, which are sung, and I will lead much of the responsive reading, which is in English. Rabbi Doug will let me read more than most of my classmates because I have a louder voice and read English well. And there is a special treat in this. I will be able to say a line that is so wonderful that it alone can draw me to Friday night services. From Psalm 98, in joyful celebration of God's creation, "Let the rivers clap hands." This falls into the leader's half of the responsive reading, and tonight I will be the leader and can finally speak these words.

In the afternoon I braid and bake challah, and it turns out well. Usually I make some mistake in the recipe and race around like the sorcerer's apprentice, leaving fingerprints of wet dough that only dynamite will remove, but as usual, shouting and panic succeed, and the product is edible. Today's bread will be for the snack after service, the *oneg*.

Julia and Jack and the grandchildren come to service, and Julia does the blessing, lighting the Sabbath candles and singing the prayer sweetly.

Leonora says, "The family has gathered, all decks on hand."

The usual forty or fifty people are at service. There is another event, a conversion. These are particularly joyful because Jews don't proselytize. In this case a young woman married into a family of concentration-camp survivors and has been swept into our beliefs. She is pregnant and lovely, and the ceremony is brief and sweet. "My first conversion," Doug tells me beforehand. "Be sure I'm here for your first exorcism," I plead. Actually I've designed three theatrical exorcisms, in Paddy Chayefsky's *The Tenth Man* and in two productions my theater has done of Ansky's play *The Dybbuk*. Imagine doing one here, in a small town in eastern Connecticut! It could pep up our fund drive.

I get through the service, speaking and singing clearly. I enjoy it, and I'm grateful for the chance to practice. Immediately after, we mill about the table at the rear of our little space and snack on the bread, plus cookies, wine and fruit juice. Mark, the only one of my classmates there this night, runs up and throws a hug around me—he's grown a few inches over the summer—and says, "Good job, big guy!" I *kvell* at the hug. I am fond of this young man and I enjoy the nickname, which, I am told by younger people, is the ultimate show of affection.

When I saw Mark's father tying his tie for him last spring, before another bar mitzvah, I was astonished at the scene, surprised that Mark didn't have all of the adult skills and surprised that he wasn't really an adult.

So what more is needed? The party is set, and I have a new jacket that I bought in Hartford. I succeeded tonight, I know how powerfully Doug will stand by me, the family has gathered, Leonora has only one more night to worry about her guest list, and my bread rose.

I'm up early on Saturday and think about my personal angels. Stand by me today! Not to pull me through my tasks, which are not so daunting, but to join me on a journey, however small, through this gateway. A journey of the spirit, it is said, and however well I deserve it, you are my spirits. Walk with me today, as through a field of wildflowers as broad and rolling as the long southern ocean. Lou Frizzel, gentle man and actor, long gone; John Coolidge, and my other teachers and friends—Ray Sovey, Jo Mielziner, Roger Furse, and Leslie Hurry; Don Oenslager, Helen Merrill. Close at my side, my mother, Sara, and my father, Mortimer. Rebecca and Margaret, their friends and then mine, and Paul. And you, with such strength, Lincoln Kirstein, but here where I can see you, not right behind me. Edith Oliver and Joe Campbell, who encouraged our theater so much; and will you be with me, Mr. B? You are my spirit, and you can't refuse me, but you never did. Sir Tyrone, marshal this crowd! Will you also lead, my beloved friend Norman Geschwind and my beloved theater partner Mack Scism? Workers with me in theater, Willy Nolan and Ron Bates; laugh at all of this, Willy, and don't sober up. Joe Layton and Dennis Scott, Frank Prince and Stark Hesseltine, lives cut short so sadly by a plague. Join me, Lena Abarbanell, who was brought to this country to create the role of Hansel at the Met, and in her later years became a scout for young talent in Harlem. I met a taxi driver in Montevideo who had known of her in Berlin. Now Leonora's dear mother, Margaret, and her husband, Bob Perlman, and Jack's father, Aaron; Jack Exton, be with me, you always blessed me with the intensity of your listening. Come along, six women in my profession whom I loved and who died in pain, Colleen Dewhurst, Joyce Ebert, Jessica Tandy, Nancy Walker, Lee Remick and Mary Martin. Mac Lowry, and Joey, aka Roger Ramsdell, master craftsman, you've all seen his work, but how many now know his name?

Hatti Brown, who was timid, such an Uncle Tom that she wouldn't sit with me on a train, and if she couldn't find a seat that was clearly worse than the others, she would stand. Will you walk proudly now? Colin Lee and Ray Harrison and Saint Subber. Pop LaRue, my athletic coach in high school, who empowered me, and his son George, lost on Okinawa, longest dead of these spirits. Dolly Haas, who told me that I had a place in heaven because I was attentive to Roger Furse when he was dying. Florence Rome, Tony Quayle, Wang Zen Tai.

I go early to the gog and help Doug set up the chairs. Rabbis are a dime a dozen, he reminds me, but a good shammes is a treasure. I then attend our Bible class, which starts at nine, an hour before the bar mitzvah. Just plain showing off, to sit serenely in class: "No blindfold, please." I excuse myself fifteen minutes early and go upstairs to greet the assembling guests, who all seem to have remained friends: Leonora's job of carpooling from New York has been a success. At ten, Rabbi Doug draws me aside and asks me to go through some parts of the service, particularly the prayers before and after the readings of the Torah and the haftorah.

The warm little room is full. That means one hundred and twenty seats, yes, all full. I'm glad to see so many friends from town who are not Jewish and have never seen this kind of a ceremony. (Rabbi to congregant, "I see you're here early to get a good seat—in the back.") When we run out of chairs, my classmates stand and offer theirs to older people. All of my classmates are here except Aaron and Rachel, but they'll get to the party. The girls have already begun to pinch and kick Adam. Doug begins the service after welcoming the crowd and encouraging those who don't know our customs to relax, clap along, anything. I'm sitting in the front row with immediate family, and my three older grandsons, with Leonora's help, put the tallit, or prayer shawl, around my shoulders. Jesse and Jordan say the blessing in Hebrew. Parents usually do that, so where are you, Mom and Dad? Should have stuck around. Leonora and I bought the tallit, and there is a matching yarmulke, but I feel more comfortable wearing the one that Max Showalter brought me from Prague. It has beautiful Hebrew letters circling it. I asked Doug to translate, and he walked around me clockwise, reading "Souvenir of Prague." Next, and the order of this may be scrambled in my memory, Doug says that he will lead a simple song, and when you're all onto the lyrics you can join in. There is only one word: "Hallelujah."

I go up on to the platform and lead the responsive reading, then sing and speak the Hebrew prayers as I did last night. I am well focused, my eye is traveling at the right speed and at the right place, just ahead of what I am speaking. These are familiar prayers, and many congregants mutter or chant or sing along with me. I have decided that I will not be dismayed if I err. I've had my ticket punched enough, I know to a reasonable extent who I am, and so do my friends, and they understand the difficulty of exact phrasing in a new language at my age. But I feel strong, my voice feels flexible and on key (it's not much of a voice, but it's not unpleasant), and I'm enough of a ham to enjoy being up in front of a crowd, of this caring crowd.

At one point in the service it is customary for the candidate's grandparents and parents to hand the Torah scroll to him or her, each touching it in turn, symbolizing knowledge going from the older to the younger generation. I suggested to Doug that my classmates could do this, and so they do, and this was seen as touching, but we were concerned about dropping it. If this happens, those who see the accident are supposed to fast for forty days, and that is why some old-timers close or cover their eyes when the scrolls move about.

We're coming to the main event, reading from the Torah and the haftorah. Suddenly I realize why I feel so healthy, so happy. All of my angels seem to be with me but they come to me now through Doug. I've made speeches or been presented with charismatic people whose fame springs from their skill but also from the power of their presence. I mean actors like Jason Robards or Zoe Caldwell. I've been in small rooms or elevators with people so electric with star quality that conversation, unless started and led by that person, was impossible: Paul Newman, Colleen Dewhurst, Christopher Dodd. I've been in an elevator with someone who needed the quality but so lacked it that we all sought to break the silence by the third floor: George McGovern. (Definition of a nebbish: when he enters a room, we think that someone's gone out.) But now, on the bema, I've never felt so powerful a human force, and it's Doug, his presence. I felt this from my son, holding me by the heel like Achilles' mother when I went into the ocean in Drake Passage, and who became almost mythic to me by the way he brought us around Cape Horn, that other Cape Horn. If I were an aerialist, would Doug be the catcher, dependably waiting for me after a triple? This is more than trust, it's transcendent faith. Nothing can go wrong with Doug beside me. Whatever is needed will happen. Simple ventriloquism? More complex, to enter me like a Dybbuk? He'll do it, and I surge forward in a feeling of sunshine and bright leaves in the clearing. I float in the beauty of the Torah, now rolled out in front of me, all of my ancestors and all of my angels aloft with me. I fight to stay on firm feet. I could rise on my toes.

Doug cries out the announcement of the Torah reading, which translated is "Be Strong!" and I put the finger of the pointer on the great hand-written letters and begin.

One is not alone on the bema. Besides Rabbi Doug a parade of friends have come up for "honors," which include saying a blessing before or after the Torah is read, or pulling the curtain to open the Ark, or passing the Torah as I've described. Wendy and Stephan, who have no Hebrew, are curtain pullers, and I'm pleased to involve that bright boy, a new family member. Now, as I start to read from the Torah, I am aware of my son-in-law's face within my vision. Jack is leaning over, looking at the section as I sing it. It is the same section he read twenty-seven years ago, one chance in sixty-seven: there are that many different passages that are used for this ceremony. A stream of sweat starts down my back as I go on. Maybe Jack doesn't realize that I have a wide field of vision. I concentrate harder than I ever have, and I sing perfectly. Maybe this was to the good, maybe I was kept from lesser distractions. Later I tell this to Jack, and rather than responding with the expected,

"Gosh, I'm sorry, I didn't realize . . ." he says that it was nothing, why, in Orthodox synagogues they all lean forward and mumble with you and correct you angrily or slap the reading stand when a mistake is made. "The Torah Police," I've heard them called. There is another point on his side. As a Jew reading the Law, I am not considered a mere speaker or a reader: I am the congregation's emissary, its representative before God. This is unique to us, to each member of a minion, and the rabbi himself has no higher station at that moment. Jack has the right, almost a duty, to read along with me, to see that I stand well for him.

The key to the ceremony, reading the Torah portion, is completed, and I sing the blessing that comes after it. Then we parade through the room with the Torah, and congregants reach out and touch it with a fringe of their prayer shawl or a corner of their prayer book. Then I sing the blessing before the haftorah. The haftorah is a far longer passage, not from the Torah, but usually from the Prophets. These sections were substituted when the Torah was forbidden to us in Roman times, and they have remained a part of this ceremony. Mine is the most beautiful of all, sheer luck that it was assigned. It comes with the date chosen for my ceremony and is linked to the Torah section. It is from Isaiah, and I read a section of it in English before starting the Hebrew. Glorious words. If you don't know them from the Bible, you may have heard them as chosen by Handel for passages in the *Messiah* (although Handel meant them differently). "Arise, shine; for thy light is come, and the glory of the Lord shines upon thee. For, behold, the darkness shall cover the earth, and fog the peoples, but the Lord shall shine upon thee, and his glory shall be seen upon thee." That's the translation given in the little blue booklet that has my particular recitations in it. Each of us in the class has a different

Torah portion and haftorah, printed in these booklets that are ordered for us when we choose our date. I chose my date because it was when our klezmer band could play.

Then I am launched into the passage, which takes almost five minutes at my speed. It may sound like chanting at first, but it is song, and I sing it with confidence and enjoyment and not as fast as my classmates, who raced through theirs. What bad can happen with Doug here? And Dan is here on the bema, on my other side, holding the heavy Torah during this long passage. His hair is purple (that bonds him with his students), and now he is worrying that it's rubbing off on the Torah. Better some Torah rub off on you, one could say, but happily I didn't become that pompous, and this magnificent man, my son, has the wisdom and kindness that study alone cannot create. Now, in the singing, I improvise a bit of tune in three or four places, and I slur two or three words. I stop at one point and say, "That wasn't good enough," and sing three words again. I know that my pronunciation is thirteen-year-old-American, but that's what I am and it sounds beautiful to me and others tell me later that it had feeling and Jack's uncle, the musician Lee Evans, says he likes my falsetto, which is needed two or three times to rescue my vocal range.

The last blessing that I make, in Hebrew, is the blessing after the haftorah. Doug made us work hard on this, and it's one of the pieces we reviewed earlier. It is contiguous to the haftorah reading, and he didn't want me to do well on that and then fail here, as kids sometimes do, and spoil it all. The home stretch. During the last phrase of this prayer Doug joins me, and then many in the congregation pick it up. The sound starts as a buzz and quickly becomes a full chorus and then, in this full room of prayer sung by the congregation, I have completed my Hebrew part of the ceremony.

Now Doug and Dan and I are dodging small missiles: my classmates are pelting us with candy. We parade the Torah through the happy room.

A final prayer for the good of Israel (the tribe, not the country) is read in English by my brother and Gene Lasko and Susan Jackson, a deaf company member, who signs her part as Julia speaks it. The language in the air is beautiful.

Doug announces my sermon, saying that when he was a student his rabbi said that the point of a bar mitzvah is not just to demonstrate knowledge acquired, but to show that one can teach. So he vowed to inflict this on his students in turn. Thus the sermon, and I divide mine into three parts. I can't resist saying that I've taught at distinguished colleges and universities, starting before Doug was born. I add that I wish I had had his patience and clarity, because I would have been a better teacher. I should have added that I would have had more humility. Then I say that I will start by thanking my teachers, because if one does not, a generational thread is broken and teaching becomes mere instruction. I name my teachers in our school and thank them, and I thank Doug, referring to a part of my haftorah, "A little one shall become a thousand," and I say how blessed all of us are in our community, people of all faiths, because he is here with us. I thank the Hormone Hurricanes and say that I'm grateful that their antics in class slowed the learning pace so that I could keep up.

I say that the second part of my sermon will be my own wisdom, and it will be brief. I say, "Today I am a boy. On the brink of manhood, to be sure, with my beloved classmates, and womanhood—more interesting. Looking back over a long life, I now understand that everything that I've done that has been fine has been done in the spirit of that boy; and everything that I've done that has been mean was done in the spirit of the man that once, so long ago, I thought it desirable to become."

The third part of my sermon, I say, will be wisdom greater than mine, and I read from *Sweet Thursday,* by John Steinbeck, and Julia comes up on the bema and signs this wonderful passage as I speak it: "The end of life is not so terribly far away. You can see it in the way you can see the finish line when you come into the stretch and your mind says, have I worked enough? Have I eaten enough? Have I loved enough? All of these, of course, are the foundation of man's greatest curse, and perhaps his greatest glory: what has my life meant so far, and what can it mean in the time left to me? And now we come to the wicked poisoned dart—what have I contributed to the great ledger—what am I worth? And this isn't vanity or ambition—men seem to be born with a debt they can never pay no matter how hard they try: it piles up ahead of them. Man owes something to man. If he ignores the debt it poisons him, and if he tries to make payments the debt only increases, and the quality of his gift is the measure of the man."

Leonora says, "There wasn't a dry seat in the house."

Doug praises me to the congregation, and I am given a certificate and a gift, a kiddush cup (which holds the wine for the Friday night blessings and for Elijah at Passover). The part of his speech that says I've done well in the ceremony was written out in advance! There are final blessings, and then Doug blesses and cuts the bread, and then we go to the party.

Chapter 23

✻   ✻   ✻

NOT FINISHED YET

P ascal in his Pensée number 555: "You would not be
looking for me if you did not possess me. So do not be
uneasy."

I visit Mark in his home. He gives me milk and cookies, and we
talk. His ceremony is over, and he did it beautifully. His sermon
was on prejudice, what else? He says he was calm and even watched
TV in the morning before going to temple. Not much and no car-
toons, he adds. He still calls me Dave, and says that it's fun not to
call me Mr. Hays. Something thrilling has happened, though this
young man seems to take it in stride. At a seniors residence in the
next town, a person who led Friday night services has become ill.
Rabbi Doug asked congregants to help them out, and he included
Mark, who will lead them soon. I wonder if Mark will berate them
for prejudice.

"To an outsider," he says, "it may look just like an ordinary relationship between a kid and his rabbi. But you know it's much more." He too felt that power and electricity on the bema, but he says he feels that whenever he is with Doug.

Does he believe in God? Without hesitation he says, "Yes. The trouble is that God isn't a He or a She. I don't buy that literal form in the Bible."

I go to Sara's house, also a home of warm and pleasant spaces. These are country houses with a plot of land, even landscaping, trees, dogs and cats. Sara and I and Jami and Rachel and Adam have something in common. We are the five out of nine in the class with two Jewish parents. Rachel's mother converted. Sara tells me that she was not as relaxed as Mark before her ceremony. She couldn't eat for three days. Also she had her school finals that same week. After these two events she had a letdown, a big drop, but it didn't last for more than a few days.

Her bat mitzvah did not alter her belief in God. Belief, yes, but again not literal. Part the Red Sea? C'mon. We talk about Mary Renault's way of describing humanly possible events that grew into great mythic literature. Yes, she knows about that, but she assures me that, like Mark, she knows that there's more to it all than Darwin. That's Einstein's belief as well. Like Einstein, she had an epiphany about God, from science. In geometry class. Pascal was a geometer. Yes, those parallel lines that will never meet. She felt from that, suddenly and powerfully, the immensity of it all.

At Adam's house I again meet his sister, a year behind us, in the big and difficult class that a certain rabbi has called "The Class from Hell." She doesn't take exception to my suggestion that it may be the most ornery class in the history of Judaism.

Adam has become taller and slimmer. He wanted to quit Hebrew school at the beginning of last year, after all the years of study, and his mother said it was up to him. Now he is teaching! He goes to class every Wednesday and helps tutor. He enjoys it. Some of the kids he coaches are "not well disciplined." Doug had reassured him that many undisciplined kids become teachers. I must agree, at least my son, Dan, has done that. "I wasn't a bad kid," says Adam. "Undisciplined, sure." He agrees with me that he would be a good choice "to be in trouble with."

Adam's grandparents were Holocaust survivors, but their son, Adam's father, had no feel for the religion. He came here from Israel at the age of eight. He married a Catholic woman and their children were raised as Catholics. Doris, his second wife and Adam's mother, was raised as a Baptist but became Jewish, not because of the marriage, but simply because she liked the religion. She was working in hospitals with many Jewish people. Her feeling is that Protestantism tells you what to do. In Judaism, at least in our version, there's interpretation. Adam adds that our holidays are so much fun. I never thought of that; Christmas and the Christmas season were such a hurdle for Jewish parents and children. But Adam cites Simhat Torah, Passover and the great autumn holidays of the New Year and Repentance. Good get-togethers, good food.

What about God? A form or a presence? Both. A problem to Adam is that all religions have their own Gods, and Adam respects them all. He has an idea that maybe we're Godlike ourselves if we can give birth to the particular form of God or the Gods we need. A heresy? Not so terrible.

Adam enjoys helping his sister with her studies. He misses the art we did and wishes we'd done more, such as painting our classroom in colors, which would have lasted for a few years. Instead, it was done for us, a plain white coating.

I ask Adam what difference he feels between his regular school and Hebrew school, and his answer is succinct. "In regular school, it's all about long-term goals that are necessary. In Hebrew school, there are no real goals unless you set them yourself." I am reminded of William Cory's address to his students at Eton, in 1861, which ends, ". . . for the art of indicating assent or dissent in graduated terms, for the habit of regarding minute points of accuracy, for the habit of working out what is possible in a given time, for taste, for discrimination, for mental courage and mental soberness. Above all, you go to a great school for self-knowledge."

I visit Aaron, whose home is on a rise in woodlands, a short walk from his school. As we talk I watch a downy woodpecker feeding only a few feet from our seats at the kitchen table. He tells me that he was most nervous at the blessing after the haftorah.

His mother is Jewish, his father is not. Did that give him a choice? "Not really," he says with a smile, "my mother makes the household rules." As to the class insubordination, he says that teachers have given up these days, they're used to it.

Aaron's God is not there for him to talk to directly, but He is there nevertheless, a holy being always around us. We need more than science, he says, we need this force. The Holocaust? That happened because so many people did not believe in God. Religious wars happened because of the opposite fervor, forgetting the Commandment "Thou shalt not kill."

Rachel, as I expected, as Doug told me to expect, is quiet and relaxed and radiant at home. Their house is on the seashore, close to the water, shoulder to shoulder with other houses. Yard space is what you give up in exchange for a front lawn that stretches to islands in the South Pacific.

Rachel felt proud after the ceremony. She had been in class for six years, starting with Rabbi Marsha, before Doug. Her father is

Jewish. Her mother converted from Protestantism, after having followed her own mother through a variety of sects. Before she converted there had been some mild but unkind remarks from one member of her husband's family, but that pressure is past.

Rachel makes the fine distinction between being nervous, which she was not, and being scared, which she was, scared of "messing up." But she felt comfortable and strong with Doug next to her. She did not feel, as did Sara, that the ceremony closed the gate on her childhood, and I expected this. Rachel's life and rhythms are more relaxed. Nor did she feel a sharp break with her graduation from Hebrew school, nor does she miss the routine. But she misses her classmates. She looked forward to seeing them each week. She does no religious work now, but may pick it up some day.

I think of my own break from The Theatre of the Deaf. What do I miss? The staff, being with them. Not much else now, after so much for so many years.

God? Yes, Rachel has always believed in God. Wouldn't I have said that at her age, after the Lionel lightbulbs? She believes in the power, the force, yes, but also has a sense, which she cannot describe, of Him as a person/presence.

In my own family, my son-in-law Jack Klebanow has become the patriarch. His father, the late and beloved Aaron, didn't want the role and never took it on, although he enjoyed the rituals, knew some Yiddish and the jokes and could heave the great shrug. Jack's outlook started on the same path as his own children, my grandchildren Jesse and Jordan and Jed, and my classmates and me. When asked, we children all say, yes, we believe in God. Later this unexamined belief can fall away. But where did we get it? Not directly from our parents. Is it built in, like our ability to acquire language, so natural and strong when we are young? When I asked Jordan why he believed, he said, "Someone created us." These children are full of the wonder of creation and indeed they are in the center of that rich act. They know that they're brand-new, that they've been created and come from somewhere, and recently. Think of their pleasure in identification with other baby animals; with chicks and ducklings and lambs and puppies and kittens. The fascinating riddle of "chicken or egg" takes their thoughts. They know that their parents arrived the same way, so they must look beyond their parents for this force. Many of them lose this mixture of curiosity and acceptance of the great unexplainable source when their minds turn to more "rational" and scientific study. Do they lose belief in God at about the age of thirteen as a part of their rebellion against their parents, who by then they understand as the procreative, even mechanical element in their creation? If they continued religious study at, say, a Catholic school, would they continue to believe? Many do not, I'm told by Catholic friends, because of stern and inflexible teachers. Their break can be sharp. Some continue, yes, because of an inspiring teacher. I found my teacher, in this arena of the spiritual, just over a year ago.

Jack is the president of the temple in Pelham Manor, which means that he examines and judges spiritual matters. His duties include the search for a new rabbi. He just sat at the head of a table set for twenty-nine at Passover, and presided with devotion over a service that he had carefully edited and could meticulously explain point by point, prayer by prayer. A year ago I asked him why he took such pleasure in the prayers if he didn't believe in God. His answer had wit: "I must admit that I do find the prayers more difficult to say in English."

Jack is not an atheist, one who denies the existence of God. Agnosticism, by one of the several definitions he knows, does not deny God but denies the possibility of truly knowing Him. Like father, like son, he says, but adds that the search could be a wonder-filled endeavor, esoteric and philosophical as much as religious. Maybe, Jack ponders, he is not agnostic, maybe he's Jewish after all.

Fear not, Jack, you're Jewish, you always were: agnostic, atheist, whatever. Just try to get out of it. Convert, like my friends and angels Lincoln Kirstein and Jo Mielziner, and you too could become known as a Jewish Catholic. What about my grandsons? They go to Hebrew school as Jack did. Like most of us, they'll take their own stance and, unlike Catholics, they'll be Jewish whether or not they have faith.

There was a skilled sailor who joined a famous yacht club, one of their first Jewish members. "But," said Leonora, "he was only half Jewish. His mother and father were Jewish, he wasn't."

Jack hangs in there: his arguments or explanations are keen. True, he doesn't pray "to" God. He prays "about" God. Religion is "the path of learning." How wonderfully Jewish! He has the usual trouble with the anthropomorphism of God; he's not happy with a God matching our image. But can we find words for a spring day, for renewal? Not really, and that, says Jack—that which is beyond words—is the realm of God. But it's all inching closer to him, he says, and what I've done has encouraged him. He continues: "Hebrew and melodies [remember, we *sing* our Bible] combine within me powerfully, bringing to my life a past that lives within me, physically and metaphorically. These songs and words are of me, of my childhood, of my past, of our past, of a history that shapes and compels us even now. The Hebrew challenges my intellect, the melodies go straight to my heart. The tangible and intangible resonate and fill me, give me that ineffable Godly aspect that unites us, commits us to one another, gives us deeds of loving kindness, gives us passion and caring for ourselves and our families and friends, and can separate us from our own petty personal needs. Sometimes."

Joseph Campbell cites an incident with a student who said that she had no personal identity without her Jewishness. He was surprised. Do you mean that I have no identity if I'm not Irish? he asked. The Patriarchs went into Egypt, says Joe. The People came out. This concept of "the People" is Near Eastern. Then Christianity followed, and it took a while for the individualism of early Europeans to rise above that collective aspect of the new religion. So he says. Yet within my religious group I see that we are strongly empowered as individuals, so much more than in many other Western religions. There is a man of coarse mentality, powerful on the synagogue building committee, who reacted to my remark that our rabbi liked such-and-such by saying, "Who cares about him? Rabbis come and go." Try that on your archbishop!

Leonora says nothing about this. Where are you when I need you?

Milk and cookies with Hannah. Her mother is Jewish, her father not. He looks like a runner, and he coaches at a high school. Her mom gives me a beautiful ceramic menorah that she has made. I can't find the tiny menorah that Dan and I used on our voyage. We had to tape it to the table in the wild southern ocean, and I have a photograph showing the candle flames at right angles to the candles. The cat walked across them and his tail ignited briefly, and Dan wondered if future generations of Hayses would light the family cat at Chanukah, a ceremony traditional to the family but with its origin lost in history.

Hannah started classes early, always assumed that she would be a bat mitzvah, and never felt coerced. She remembers her comment about God being impossible because there was the Holocaust, but she won't decide that yet. You know, she says, at my age one has a tendency to go along with the last person, the last idea, that we hear. In her eloquent sermon she spoke of the rules we need for our lives. Her text from the Bible was pre-Sinai, before the Commandments, when God Himself was changing the rules as if He Himself was learning.

Jami's home is also airy and relaxed. She too started early, in kindergarten, and she remembers that all matters relating to the school moved ahead with vigor when Doug came to us. She went twice to Hebrew camp, one week one summer, two weeks the next. No pressure, she felt it to be a thing one does. She says that she was bored by some of our class activities, but not Hebrew itself. She says that she's not idealistic, by which I believe she means that she's realistic. The example that she gives is that if she's hurt she knows that she will be in pain and moody and snap at people. No Polyanna, Jami. And she says that she knows that she's still a kid. She was before and she is now. No "gateway" for her.

She felt that she achieved her goal in the ceremony and that's that. She has no current plans to continue study. The Hormone Hurricanes didn't make her bat mitzvah ceremony easy, she says. They held their prayer books upside down, and her brother made faces. Par for the course, she wasn't singled out. I do remember that she laughed once up on the bema, but like the other kids, she got through it all "without messing up," in fact with dignity. She remembers what I said about her on the bema.

She says that most of the time she doesn't believe in God. But sometimes she does. People make unexpected recoveries from surgery, for example. "I believe in God in life-and-death situations," she says.

And me, bar mitzvah boy? What have I learned from this complex year and the strings, suddenly brought into focus, that attached it to my past years, to my earliest memories? Has there been an "event"? Perhaps. There's a road in Maine, Route 9, going east from Augusta to Calais, a town on the border of Canada. I recently drove to Nova Scotia to spend time with Dan and his family, living then in the cabin we built. There is a steep hill just before Calais, and as I drove up I caught the blazing sunset in all three mirrors. I stopped at the top and stepped out to look. An eighteen-wheeler was crawling up the hill, so slowly, and I made aircraft-docking circles with my hands and laughed with the driver as he crept past, and then I stood and watched the sky.

A week later I drove home to Connecticut. I made the border by dark, stayed at a motel, and started again at dawn. At the crest of that same hill I caught the blazing red sunrise, now behind me, in all three mirrors. It glowed on the tops of the firs ahead. I stopped again and stepped out to watch. Come on—what do you want! Maybe I cried, just a little. Not big stuff. The air smelled so sweet. On that dusty road, I wonder, did I step across that line between "Prove that there is a God," to "Prove that there isn't"?

There is another way, call it another translation, to state the thought by Pascal that began this chapter. "If you're looking for God, you've found Him." Found whom? Do I start to pay attention to the man behind the curtain?

If Joseph Campbell says that the Patriarchs went into Egypt and came out the People may I, not exactly a patriarch, go into a year with Rabbi Doug and the Hormone Hurricanes and my Young

Lady and come out a Child, or almost a Child? Can I pick up, once again, that understanding of creation as a child understands it, even as I wear my barnacles and carry my lifetime baggage? Can we cut out those middle years and hear the bells again, in the quiet evening air?

During this past year with Rabbi Doug and my classmates, have I become committed to the search? A search with an objective? I'm not sure about the objective, but I know the voyage. I've signed on again, on board as I was when a boy, and I am not uneasy. Walking to the Lunch Box, I watch the sunrises more closely, the way that the concerned mariner studies them for news. Not for news of Him or Her in person. But I can now read with more understanding the great book that He wrote, or helped us write, and I can read with more understanding the fascinating and instructive stories. Does He expect more of me than that? All things, as made by Darwin and Senior Partner, Ltd., have been dusted off. I have become a boy again. The search is frustrating when I expect more than I can understand anyway.

Leonora says, "David's had a revision."

It's as simple as that, and I'll try to stick around, Jordan. In the meanwhile, like Hillel, I can stand on one foot and recite the great rule, the Golden Rule, and say, yes, all the rest is commentary. I'm learning, like Akiva. Slowly.